THE 1%

FINDING HOPE AGAINST ALL ODDS

By

Julie Brown

ISBN: Paperback 978-1-963679-63-2

Hardback 978-1-963679-64-9

Dedication

Dedicated to my mom, Kathleen Smith, and Tom's mom, Ellen Brown, two ladies who shaped our lives and taught us to love unconditionally.

Acknowledgments

Starting my appreciation with the one and only for me - Tom – my ROCK! Your positivity never wavered. You stepped up and advocated for me in every way you could, and that saved me! From the day I met you, you have always been my biggest fan, so no surprise you were with me every step of the way on this journey! I love you and appreciate the amazing partner you are in my life!

I look forward to every new memory we will make!

To my kids and their supportive partners - Courtney & Kenny, Megan & Nick, Luke & Natalie. You have always been my motivation to do well in life. Thank you for taking the role of motivator and caregiver while I was in need. Seeing a parent in that condition hits you at your core, but you showed everyone what you were made of and stood strong. Your support of your dad and being with him when I couldn't be meant the world to me. My love for you is never-ending, and I'm so proud of all of you.

To my perfect and sweet grandkids - Lola, Knox, Lincoln & Violet (and now Josie, who wasn't born until after this journey) – you gave me a reason to recover! Watching you grow with each picture and video made me more determined to get out of the hospital and be a part of those moments! Always know you have the ability in you to do whatever you want! Grandma & Pap love you dearly!

To my brothers and sisters and in-laws - Sue & Pat, Lori & Dave, Andy & Belinda, Karen & Barry and Ed & Robbie – mom and dad taught us all to stick together in all we do. I couldn't ask for a better family – period! Sue/Lori/Karen – how lucky am I to have three best friends as sisters?! Ed and Andy – you have always been my biggest protectors! I'm sure watching me go through this and not being able to make it better killed all of you, but know, your words of wisdom and faith encouraged me along the way, and your love was felt every day!

To Gina & Billy - thank you for opening your home to Tom most nights for home-cooked meals, a shoulder to lean on and an ear to listen. You know him best, and being able to talk to you about what he was going through was the best medicine for him.

An extra special thanks to my sister Sue. She talked with Tom daily and started the communication email that kept everyone informed on my progress. She and Tom spent a lot of time each day working through what to say and this created the base for this book. You also stepped in as Tom's "voice of reason", and for that, we are both forever thankful.

To my book proofreaders – Courtney, Megan, Sue, Lori, Karen, Natalie, Gina, Angie and Aunt Jeanne. You saw the process early on and gave me great feedback to get me to this point. Thanks!

To the long list of friends, family and community members who brought meals to our home for four months after my return home. You spoiled us with amazing cooking and made me up my cooking game ever since! Thank you for your charity and the love you brought into our home. Thanks to my sister Karen for organizing this list!

To our in-home care providers. Erin, my nurse, you were not here long, but you were so compassionate – thank you. To my physical therapist, Deena – your over-the-top personality and your own story of fighting was exactly what I needed. You motivated me to break through so many barriers, physically and emotionally, and I am forever in your debt! And to my occupational therapist, Barb – from day one, you had me pushing to do day to day tasks and made it easier to transition to living at home. My work with all of these "friends" made a difference in my recovery. I will always cherish our work together!

To my outpatient physical and pulmonary rehab therapist – I was blessed to find two groups of compassionate yet aggressive therapists who had my best interest in mind. Thank you for pushing me to walk without assistance and strengthening my muscles! I never liked exercise, but I always looked forward to getting out to see you each day, so that in itself is a compliment!

To my family & friends who took the time to visit me at each hospital. I know those visits to see me could not have been easy (and probably left a few mental scars!). I looked forward to every one of those visits and treasured our alone time together! Thanks for encouraging me and giving me words of wisdom to believe in my recovery.

To everyone who sent cards, gift cards, emails and texts to myself, Tom and my family during our darkest hours. Your generosity and love carried Tom and me through and confirmed our belief that we have a village of faith and love around us!

To my niece Alexis, for creating the beautiful cover for this book. You are very talented and were patient with my ever-changing mind to find the perfect image I was looking for! Thank you!

To the team of people who helped pull off the fundraiser of all fundraisers! Special thanks to my cousin Rose & Ken for your generous contribution and hard work that day, The KofC for the use of their facility and donation and my wonderful family and friends who planned, organized and ran this very special day. Thanks also to all the people and companies who donated money or baskets. And lastly, to my cousin Ruth & Ab for running the Texas Hold 'em tournament. Tom and I were so humbled by everyone's generosity, and the atmosphere of the day was pure love.

To the entire staff at all five hospitals, in particular the ECMO team, the amazing 4SW team, my long-term rehab team of hope (Bill, Tim, Dr. C, Tasha), and my in-hospital rehab group (Alli and Bobbie). The sacrifices you all made during the COVID pandemic to bravely face the unknown and show up every day to save lives will never be forgotten. Thank you for never giving up on me and all the other patients! You were my family when they couldn't be with me. I am forever grateful for your expertise.

And lastly, to my prayer warriors. Without your constant faith, hope and love, I truly do not feel I would have had the strength to fight. Believe in prayer and believe in miracles – they are all around us! Thank you for your unending prayers, and I promise I will pay them forward!

About the Author

Julie Brown never set out to be a writer. Life had other plans - a twist of fate that unfolded during her battle with COVID-19. Now, with unwavering courage, she stands ready to share her rollercoaster of a journey with the world.

Born and raised in the small town of Hanover, PA, Julie spent many years immersed in the manufacturing world, focusing in finance and supply chain roles. She is a devoted wife, a proud mother of 3 kids and a doting grandmother to 5 grandkids. Her greatest pleasure lies in the simple moments; playing cards, spending time with family and friends and occasionally testing her luck at the casino.

In this debut memoir, *The 1%, Finding Hope Against All Odds*, Julie writes in a personal and relatable style, capturing the isolation, resilience and hope that defined her fight. The story is a testament of survival and a celebration of a life reclaimed. Her path reminds us all that sometimes the most profound stories emerge from unexpected chapters of life.

Contents

CHAPTER 1
A DAY TO REMEMBER

Wednesday, November 24, 2021, will forever hold a special place in my heart. It was the day I finally went home from the hospital. As soon as I woke up, I was super pumped up with excitement. There were no mixed emotions on this day! The hospital had become my temporary home, with its clean walls and busy halls, but nothing felt as good as being back home, cozy and comfortable. I couldn't wait to go home to be with my family, sleep with my husband in our bed and see my grandkids!

Finally, the moment came. With excitement and hope, I was heading home. The journey had its harrowing moments, but with each mile, I felt happier. And suddenly, there I was, at my doorstep – where love and warmth awaited me. My family had a homecoming planned that was fit for a queen! Since early morning, my sisters worked to turn our home into a place of happiness and celebration. They used balloons, homemade signs filled with memories, and lots of streamers to make it feel like a grand party fit for royalty.

My husband Tom woke up that morning and felt that the light at the end of the tunnel was upon us. That day ranked up there with our wedding day and the birth of our kids. He said seeing the excitement in my sisters' eyes when they arrived at our house was like seeing kids on Christmas morning. The joy was overwhelming. Looking at the decorations in our home, Tom couldn't help but think about the challenging journey we had been through to get here. It was a journey filled with uncertainty and fear, but most importantly, it was a journey guided by constant love and support. This was a feeling of unconditional love, and it felt amazing. When you don't know if you'll get a second chance at living with your love, knowing you are getting her back just makes a living even better.

As my sisters added the finishing details to the decorations, my nephew Bubba captured every moment with his camera. The excitement in the air was tangible. They couldn't contain their joy as they saw the elegant limousine arrive at our doorstep, a sign of the grand celebration awaiting us on this special day.

Filled with excitement and beaming smiles, my sisters, along with Tom and Bubba, joyfully climbed into the limousine, their laughter spreading infectious happiness. As they set off to pick me up from the hospital, they chatted about the ups and downs of the past year – a whirlwind of emotions and obstacles that had brought us to this happy moment. They FaceTimed me so I could get a taste of the excitement headed my way. Bubba was enjoying the experience in the limo, videotaping the shenanigans as well as coordinating with different news stations who were planning on covering the story as I arrived home. As the hospital came into sight, Tom said we were coming to take his love home. The anticipation of what was to come next was incredible.

At the hospital entrance, my sisters joined a gathering crowd of staff, sharing Tom's anticipation. With each minute, their excitement heightened, knowing that our reunion was approaching. As Tom walked down the hall to my room, he was reveling in the glory of the moment. The hair on the back of his neck was standing up with excitement. It was a WOW moment. He had walked through hospital halls alone for months, and this time, he'd be walking out with me to take me home. It was a dream come true.

Once we exited the hospital and loaded into the limo, the party began! Champagne was popping, and food was coming around plate after plate. We listened to music and drank, ate and talked non-stop. Bubba continued videoing the experience, celebrating with us as well as keeping in touch with the news outlets, who were already gathering at our house. My kids, Courtney, Luke and their families were at home welcoming the groups of news crews, family and friends who were waiting for my arrival home. The atmosphere was so upbeat!

The road to get to this day was a roller coaster - a COVID coaster if you will! This book is about the journey that led up to this celebration. Sit back and get ready for an unbelievable journey that took me to the brink of death and back - twice, and the amazing story of a positive, loving and supportive team of people who wouldn't let me fail!

CHAPTER 2
BLISSFULLY UNAWARE

My name is Julie Brown, downtown Julie Brown to many of my friends and family! I have been married for over 25 years to the love of my life, Tom. We have three kids we share together: a son, Luke and two daughters, Megan and Courtney. They are all grown up and living on their own, so we were enjoying our empty nester period of life! At that time, we had four grandkids, which we saw often and thoroughly enjoyed. I grew up with a family of 6 kids - Ed, Karen, Andy, Lori, and Sue with me being the youngest child. My father, Elmer, passed away in 2004 after many years of battling with emphysema and blood cancer. His courageous battle and the manner in which he fought has been an inspiration to all of us. My mother, Kathleen, was a dedicated housewife who babysat kids in her house for years. Once Dad passed away, she surprised us with her independence and strength to live on her own after many years of being right by Dad's side. Tom comes from a smaller family. His mom, Ellen, and his father, Jim, separated early in his life. He grew up with his mother and two sisters, Gina and Angie, with visits to their dad's house.

Tom and I have both been born, raised and reside in the same 2-mile area of the world! We have both been at our employers for many years. Tom is a manager at a brick manufacturer, and he has been there for 30 years. I am a supply chain manager for a window manufacturer, and I have been at my company for 22 years. Commitment in all aspects of our life is important to us.

We had built together what we considered to be a great life. We enjoy following our favorite sports teams. Tom has been a lifelong Detroit Lions and Houston Astros fan as well as all things racing! I turned him from following Miami Hurricanes to Penn State Nittany Lions very early in our relationship! I am a Nittany Lion and Dallas Cowboys superfan. We have a strong circle of friends and family we see often. My health has been good over the years. I had high blood pressure, but who doesn't after raising three kids and working a high-pressure job for so many years? Tom has had more health problems in life, including diabetes and three back surgeries. The thought of a pandemic popping up and changing our lives was the furthest thing from our minds.

The first time we heard about COVID was on an annual trip we took down to Ocean City, Maryland, for St. Patrick's Day weekend. This was in March of 2020. My husband Tom and I were sitting at the Jetty Restaurant on the Bay with some of our dearest friends from high school, and we were watching the news of what was changing with the NCAA for March Madness. We were all discussing how crazy limiting spectators seemed. How could a sickness be so contagious that such extreme measures are required? We started realizing how much we didn't know about the virus. While down at Ocean City that weekend, we visited some of our favorite bars and heard from the bar talk that schools were shutting down and restaurants were limiting capacity. The annual parade for St. Patrick's Day was canceled in Ocean City. The CDC recommended people start distancing themselves 6 feet apart from others and use hand sanitizer to help kill the virus. It was just the beginning of something we had no idea was going to get as big as it was. We enjoyed our weekend with caution and went back to our normal lives.

As the weeks progressed, companies that were deemed 'non-essential' were requested to shut down to try to limit the spread of COVID-19. Tom's company shut down for several weeks. My company stayed open but had management take a 2-week furlough. Reactions to a virus had never caused shutdowns or precautions like this in our lifetime, so the guidelines definitely had our attention. Tom and I did what we could to limit our exposure to others. We both had elderly parents who needed our help from time to time. We were very cautious as we went into their homes to see them. We stopped the visits we had with our kids and grandchildren which was so hard to do. The demand for cleaning items and essential household supplies increased. The first commodity that became scarce in stores was toilet paper. We went on a mad scramble from store to store, looking to get any toilet paper we could find! We found a generic brand, but that is just not a commodity you want to sacrifice quality on if you know what I mean! Thankfully, we had a friend who had extra good brand toilet paper, so we got a mega pack from them!

As the months progressed in 2020, we stopped our weekly family get-togethers at my mom's house on Sunday nights. Our first family visit to see my mom was on Easter. Our family made a personalized video sending well wishes and love from each family member. My sisters Karen, Lori, Sue, and I went to her house to show it to her. We spread out in the kitchen, of course with our mask on, and watched the video with her. She loved it! The toll of not seeing loved ones in person during the pandemic was enormous. That day, Tom and I also delivered Easter baskets to each of our kids' houses. We put the baskets at the end of the driveway and talked to the kids outside. Not hugging our grandkids was nearly impossible that day!

On Mother's Day, my three sisters and two brothers, along with our spouses and kids, all met in the backyard of Mom's house. We stood 6 feet apart and enjoyed seeing everyone in person. We needed to be together and feel our family bond, but mostly, we needed to see Mom so badly. Mom beamed from ear to ear looking around at her family she had missed seeing together. It was a good day for all of us.

We decided to continue with our yearly family beach vacation. We went to Sandbridge Beach, close to Virginia Beach. My three sisters and I have taken our families to the beach together for over 20 years. But this year, we only had about half the kids come with us due to COVID concerns. As with everything else during this period, it was fun but just not the same as before.

In September, I celebrated my 50th birthday. Since new cases of COVID had somewhat stabilized, I went to the casino with my sister Karen, brother-in-law Barry and my brother Ed. We enjoyed the day doing one of our favorite activities, playing the slots, and then headed back to my house. When we pulled up, there was a lawn full of family and friends waiting to celebrate my birthday with me! This was the first party Tom had ever planned by himself, and he did a great job surprising me. We had great food, lots of pictures and memories with old friends.

We also joined the bandwagon of shut-in families and added a dog to our household. We named him Logan. We got him from a rescue that picked up dogs from Louisiana right before Hurricane Laura hit them. He was two months old and a mix of a labrador and what we think was a Catahoula. He has a ton of energy and loves to play. We had two other dogs that both passed away, so it was a hard decision to start over with another dog, but we were so happy we did.

Many traditional gatherings stopped that year as well. No family reunions, no Halloween parties, and reduced Christmas and New Year's Eve gatherings. Tom and I had purchased a 1982 Corvette the prior year. To fill our free time, we started taking long drives in the Corvette. We also repainted a room in the house, refinished furniture and stained the deck. You must get creative when looking for entertainment and things to do during a pandemic. Sometimes, slowing life down and appreciating your home and family is not such a bad thing.

As 2021 started, we were hoping for a better year. Unfortunately, Tom started having pain in his neck in January. He went to see a new back doctor who sent him to physical therapy. He had to stop working because of the physical nature of his job. It became more difficult and painful to hold his head up. His hands were going numb, and he was losing feeling in his arms. He went to one session of rehab before life threw us a curveball.

Our Family

CHAPTER 3
BECOMING A STATISTIC

In past centuries, viruses would take a long time to spread. With today's advances in transportation, the speed at which viruses infect worldwide has accelerated significantly, putting us all at a greater risk. Cities have become more populated, making a perfect environment for the rapid spread of diseases. We've experienced a few epidemics/pandemics in the past century. In 2009, the H1N1 flu virus, also known as the Swine flu pandemic, spread worldwide. I remember that virus, but honestly, the impact on our lives was minimal. Some people were getting the swine flu vaccine, but we chose not to get it for our kids or us.

In the early 1980's, the human immunodeficiency virus, or HIV, was detected. HIV is spread through blood or by sex. It attacked the immune system and, in some cases, progressed to AIDS. I was a teenager during the original outbreak. We really weren't concerned about changing anything in our lifestyle except practicing safer sex practices! In 1918, the Spanish flu pandemic was another H1N1 flu virus. We obviously weren't around for that one, but I had read about the widespread disease and how many people died worldwide. All the above are pandemics I am blessed to say did not affect my family, but I'm sure other families can write a novel like I am about their experiences with the virus.

In December 2019, the world was introduced to SARS-CoV-2, otherwise known as COVID-19. Within two months, the outbreak was declared a pandemic. The scariest part of this virus was the lack of early information on how it was spread and who was at the highest risk.

February 19, 2021, was the end of a normal work week for me. I had a 2-hour meeting with my coworker in my office that afternoon. He had some minor cold symptoms that day but nothing that concerned either of us. We were both masked and sitting across a desk from each other. We finished the meeting, and I wrapped up work and headed home for the weekend. During that weekend, I felt fine. I watched my two grandsons, Knox and Lincoln, on Saturday morning while my son, Luke and my daughter-in-law, Natalie, worked. Tom and I went out to dinner with our friends Bill and Wendy on Saturday night. After dinner, we stopped over at my sister Karen's house and hung out with her and her husband Barry and my nephew Ryan. On Sunday, my daughter Courtney came over to our house, and I taught her how to file her taxes online. We went to my mom's home that night. My sisters, brothers-in-law and some of our nieces and nephews would come to Mom's house weekly to talk, laugh and visit with her each week. We all sat around her kitchen table that night with our masks on, talking and eating, but not all were distanced 6 feet apart as we should have been. A relative had requested Mom's legendary fudge, and we were trying to figure out how to make it (something she used to know by heart, but her mind was slipping as she aged). The fudge didn't set well, so we all dug our spoons into the remains and enjoyed how good it tasted. When leaving, while still being masked, I gave Mom a hug and a kiss and told her that I loved her. This night would become a significant memory for me, but I had no idea of its importance at the time.

On Monday morning, when I got to work, I received a call from my coworker that his cold had gotten worse over the weekend. He had tested positive for COVID. He said he was not feeling well at all and was hospitalized with pneumonia the next day. As with our policy, I left work right away and quarantined, although I had no symptoms. On Tuesday morning, I drove to my doctor's office and got a COVID test. The nurse came out to my car to administer a rapid test. Within a few minutes, I received my results - I was positive for COVID-19. It's very surreal when you get that positive result, even if you don't feel bad. It's like you are now part of this pandemic group - you are a statistic! That afternoon, I started getting a fever, sore throat, body aches and chills.

By Wednesday, Tom started getting mild cold symptoms and a fever. He did not get a COVID test, feeling it was redundant to get one, knowing he lived with someone who had just tested positive. At the time, there was no at-home test kit for COVID, so if you wanted to be tested, you had to go to a testing center or your doctor's office. Hospitals did not want to see you unless they knew your COVID status. Tom did, however, start quarantining immediately. My cold symptoms started getting worse and the sickness went to my chest. I called my doctor on Thursday, and she told me to use over-the-counter medicines to treat my symptoms as well as ordered a prescription cough medicine, Tessalon Perles. She also told me to get a pulse ox monitor and watch my oxygen levels. If my oxygen saturation went below 92%, I was to go straight to the hospital. My sister Lori, who worked at a pharmacy, got a pulse ox for me and delivered it to the house that day.

My daughter, Courtney and my sister, Karen, also tested positive on Wednesday. We created a text group called "the COVID gang" and we were communicating back and forth on how we were doing. I felt bad that I was the first one to have it, and I felt that I had spread it to others in my family, but it was nice to go through it with others to compare symptoms and give advice on what may help.

By Friday, I was still getting worse, and my oxygen level went down to 92%. That day, I made my first visit to the emergency room at our local hospital. They checked me over and gave me a breathing treatment. They also did a chest x-ray and said I did not have pneumonia. Since my oxygen saturation was good on room air, they said I should go home and continue doing the same routine treatment that I was doing. I was a bit frustrated as I was feeling horrible with a nasty cough, and the staff couldn't do much more than send me home and let the virus run its course.

Saturday morning, I woke up without a fever for the first time since Tuesday. I was excited to get my first positive step since I got my diagnosis. Our newest addition, Logan, decided to chew up our pulse ox monitor, so I had to borrow one from my sister until I could get a new one! The excitement from having no fever was short-lived as later that afternoon, my fever came back, and I developed a crackling in my lungs, and I couldn't take a deep breath.

By Sunday morning, my breathing was much worse. I went back to our local hospital emergency room. They checked me out more thoroughly this time. They did a chest X-ray and said that I now had pneumonia. They gave me IV fluids and ran some bloodwork. I was given a choice of whether to stay in the hospital or go home. I had oxygen saturations between 94% and 97% on room air without oxygen aid, so I chose to go home. I did get an inhaler to help with my breathing, as well as a steroid. As the day progressed, I lay on the couch, coughing more and more. I started having bladder control issues, which I thought was just from coughing so violently. Tom had suggested I go back into the hospital, but I was fighting back that I didn't want to go back twice in one day and pay another visit fee.

Monday morning introduced fresh hurdles as I consulted my family doctor through a video call. Despite the discomfort of my persistent cough, the doctor assured me that it signaled my body's efforts to fight off pneumonia. However, the pain in my rib cage served as a reminder of the strain the coughing was putting on me.

Feeling desperate, I asked about getting a plasma infusion to help my recovery, but I found out it was only for hospitalized patients. Despite this disappointment, my doctor encouraged me, saying my body could overcome this challenge with patience and time.

As the day passed, I battled with the relentless coughing, trying every cough medicine I could find to ease my discomfort. Throughout the night, I carefully monitored my pulse ox levels, knowing how crucial it was to keep my oxygen levels stable while fighting pneumonia.

Despite the hurdles ahead, I held onto the hope that every cough was a sign of progress toward recovery. As I prepared for another uncomfortable night, I wondered when the medicine was going to kick in and I would start feeling better.

On Tuesday, March 2, I felt like I couldn't breathe at all. On a very cold, early AM hour, we went back to our local hospital emergency room for a third time. At that point, they admitted me. After a few tests, they took me straight to the intensive care unit (ICU). I had developed COVID double pneumonia. I was diagnosed with acute hypoxemic respiratory failure, which is a lack of oxygen in my blood. My hospital journey had begun!

CHAPTER 4
LEARNING PATIENCE

"To lose patience is to lose the battle." ***Mahatma Gandhi***

Day one in the hospital was extremely chaotic for me. The room was full of nurses and doctors asking me a million questions about my health. I had a urinary tract infection, which explained my uncontrolled bladder functions, so they treated me for that immediately. I was coughing more and more and couldn't clear my chest. They started me on steroids, antibiotics, and inhalers, among other medicines, to start treating my symptoms. I was put on high-flow oxygen through a nasal cannula in my nose. I was still able to eat regular food. However, eating with high-flow oxygen through your nose was not an easy task!

Tom was not allowed to be with me in the ICU for the first few days because he was still sick with COVID-19 symptoms. Since he was quarantined, he went home and started making calls to inform our kids and families that I was admitted to the hospital. His sinuses were burning, he was extremely tired and had body aches, so he got some much-needed rest that day.

They put me in a COVID isolation room. There was a large and very loud ventilation machine that filtered the air in the room. I seriously thought I might go deaf from that machine; it was excessively loud! How was someone supposed to rest with that in the room? Anyone going in and out of the room had to put on a plastic gown, mask and gloves. Leaving the room, they needed to take off their gown and sanitize so no germs left the room with them.

I had a great staff of doctors who were working all avenues to help my condition improve. I received convalescent plasma to help boost my immunity to the virus. I also received Remdesivir antiviral medication. I was hypotensive (meaning low blood pressure), so they started me on

IV fluids and Levophed to help with my low blood pressure. I requested for the doctors to look up any new trials they were hearing about amongst other facilities. One of the doctors found a drug called Tocilizumab, which was a drug used to treat rheumatologic disorders but was found to help severe COVID-19 patients. Tom fought with the insurance company and got approval for the treatment. I was the first at our local hospital to receive this drug.

The nurses started me on a technique called proning. Proning is where you lay on your stomach instead of your back. This helps you breathe better by giving better drainage of secretions from the lungs as well as taking the compression off the lungs and abdomen, helping with gas exchange in the lungs. I lay in this position for as many hours as I could, but it became very uncomfortable. This is when I started having my first anxiety attacks. Lying on your stomach is not a pleasant position when you can't breathe. I would try to pass the time by listening to music, but I kept finding I didn't have the patience to lie like that for too long. You could not watch TV or read because of the position you were in, so distractions were not easy to find. Any visitors would rub my back for the entire time they were there to help me relax. Somehow I got through as many as 16 hours a day of proning, but it was a struggle. The nurses were telling me the patients who could tolerate laying like this were giving their lungs a chance to improve, so I was determined to do it, whether I liked it or not.

Tom was overwhelmed with emotion and heartbroken over my illness. His initial thoughts were, why couldn't it be him and not me? He posted on Facebook for our friends to pray for me. Our friends responded in full force and all started praying. This also prompted many calls, messengers and text messages asking what was wrong and asking for updates. This put additional stress on Tom as he was struggling to talk about it. This was on top of his recovery from COVID-19 symptoms and neck pain he was experiencing. He started turning his phone off and secluding himself to bed to rest and process his emotions.

At this point, I was alert and knew most of what was going on. They continued to use different techniques to help me breathe. They started using a BiPAP machine on me at night time. For a claustrophobic person like myself, this was a tough adjustment. BiPAP is a mask they put over your nose and mouth and force air through your airways to help you breathe better. I asked to have anxiety medicine before I went to sleep to help me relax before the respiratory therapist put the mask on. I would wake up in the morning in a panic because it was strapped to my head, and I couldn't get it off. One morning I FaceTimed Tom in a full-fledged panic attack. I couldn't talk to him because I had the mask on, but I was just pointing in the phone and he somehow understood right away that I needed him. He came to the hospital quickly and helped settle me down. Thank God by this time, they were allowing Tom to visit for a short time. My room was right by the nurse's station, so I could flag down a staff member quickly if I needed help, and they were so attentive to my needs. I quickly started building relationships with staff members who were so sympathetic to what I was going through.

Of the nine people who were at my mom's house on that fateful Sunday night, six people tested positive with COVID the next week. My daughter, husband, sister, brother-in-law and nephew. Most of them had mild symptoms and got through it fine. Unfortunately, the person that I least wanted to affect was my mother, and she had gotten it as well.

Mom got diagnosed with COVID a few days after I did. My brothers and sisters took care of her at home before she was admitted to our local hospital on March 7, 2021, less than a week after I was admitted. She started off in a regular room. Her breathing condition worsened, and within a day, she was transferred to the intensive care unit. The day after that, she was put on a ventilator.

I knew Mom had tested positive for COVID-19, as I was in touch with her on how I was feeling before I went into the hospital. But once I found out mom was advanced to intensive care, I asked my family not to give me updates on her, as I was not in a mental state to be able to handle any bad news about her. Tom said I made a snide comment that I bet mom was getting better nights of sleep than I was since she was on a ventilator and sedated, and I was struggling to breathe and awake each night. My mom was not told that I was in the hospital. This made it tricky for the people visiting us, as our rooms were side by side, and we could see straight out to the nurses' station. My family pleaded for our rooms not to be close together, but unfortunately, that hospital only had 2 COVID isolation rooms in the ICU, so she was put in the room right beside mine. The number of people visiting was extremely limited due to the COVID restrictions. At this point, only two people per patient were allowed to visit. I would get nervous every time I saw doctors and nurses running past my room because I would always think something had happened to Mom. I would try to sit quietly in my room and see if I could hear what was going on in her room or hear her voice, but I couldn't. I would listen to what the nurses were talking about to see if they'd let something slip about how she was. I was left to just pray non-stop for her as well as my recovery. Little did I know that the entire staff was informed about our family situation and knew not to say a word about what was going on in the other room.

At my work, a double-digit number of people tested positive for COVID the same week I did, one being my son, Luke, who worked closely with me each day. With most of my main family members, all quarantined for COVID and mom now in the hospital and needing visitors, my main supporter for a visitor for the first few days was my sister Sue. The rest of my very close family could only communicate through emails and phone calls, but mostly worried and prayed at home. Sue did a great job getting everything I needed and helping to calm me while she was there. She asked what she could do to help us. I knew that Tom was getting bombarded by everyone to get updates on my condition. I asked her to take a load of channeling communications through her to help Tom. She started an email chain to give daily updates to everyone on how I was doing. This was a huge help for Tom and quickly became a blessing to everyone getting the email.

When Tom and our daughter, Courtney, got out of their quarantine time, they became my rotating visitors and Sue took over helping care for our mom. When Courtney visited, I had great conversations with her about how to handle my anxiety, as that is something she struggled with in her life. She gave me key words she wrote on the wall to help me focus on when I was alone and struggling. What a role reversal to see my youngest child now teaching me how to handle a life issue! Tom always wrote words of encouragement on my board to make me feel better. His presence would always calm me down, and my vital signs would always improve when he was in the room. Unfortunately, anxiety had become an everyday problem for me, and I was not handling it well. The crazy part was that I had never had anxiety a day in my life before this illness.

Tom was still dealing with his neck pain that had started at the beginning of the year. He was sent for an MRI to better understand the extent of his injury. He had two displaced discs. One was pressed against the spinal cord, which the doctor was very concerned about, and the other was pressed against a bundle of nerves. It affected the use of his left arm. He would come in to see me every day, although he was in significant pain himself. He had a hard time keeping his head up for the few hours he visited.

As the week progressed, my breathing continued to deteriorate. I remember looking up on the internet relaxation techniques and ways to calm yourself. I practiced everything I found that would help me. I turned to prayer every waking moment I had. One night, as I was looking out the window late at night, I saw an image of a young boy sitting in a tree. I immediately identified him as what my dad, who passed away 16 years prior, looked like in his early-age pictures. He just smiled and watched over me - it was a relaxing feeling to know he was there. I asked all my family and friends to pray for me. Pray that I could get better; pray that I would stop having anxiety; pray that this would not be a long-lasting illness and that I would be back on my feet soon. I started getting piles of e-cards through the hospital portal. I was getting text messages from good friends and relatives who were finding out I was in the hospital and deteriorating. This is when I first realized I was not alone in this battle and started feeling the army of supporters I had in my life. When sitting in a hospital room alone, many thoughts go through your head, and those moments of getting a card or text may be all you need at that moment to get you through.

Getting through the night was very hard because there were few distractions, and sleep was not happening. I remember one night, I listed everyone in my family and, in my head, one by one, asked them to take a breath for me. It helped me get my mind off my breathing issue and supplied a little humor when I got to certain people! I came to a point where I couldn't take the fight anymore, and during my prayers, I told God I was in his hands because I just couldn't do it anymore. During those prayers, I heard a deep, calming voice say something to me that relaxed me. For the life of me, I can't remember what he said, but I remember I settled right away and fell asleep. Putting your problems in God's hands and trusting that he has you is something I never really did before that point in life.

I was fighting each night I had the BiPAP mask. One night, I made it my goal to keep it on all night. I woke up at 6 am and willed myself to keep it on until 7 am when the nursing staff switched. I was so proud of myself that I hit my goal. Then, I had a huge panic attack that was bad enough for the doctor to be called in. They were yelling out all kinds of stat commands - morphine, lasix, blood work - they were able to calm me down for a moment. Still, again, the nurses had to call Tom to calm my nerves because I just couldn't shake the jitters. I was so scared! That's the roller coaster of ups and downs COVID-19 plays with your head. People who were not even as sick as me were dying. People who were younger than me were dying. As I lay in bed getting sicker and sicker, and the doctors were advancing my dependence on machines and medicine, it was hard not to think this might be the end of my life on Earth.

I was getting very edgy with the people closest to me. My son Luke sent me a text message asking when I was getting out of the hospital. I sent a very direct message back to him explaining this was a long haul and that he needed to educate himself with Courtney and Tom on how sick I actually was. Then I told him how hard it was for someone like me to be happy with baby steps, and my biggest achievement that day was having a bowel movement! My sister, Karen, sent me a message saying this recovery would be a breeze, and I barked back at her that nothing about this journey was easy and I was tired of taking baby steps. The stress of the proning, anxiety, inability to breathe and overall feeling bad was getting the best of me. I didn't go into the hospital being a patient person, but I quickly learned that things were out of my control, and I needed to learn patience to get through it. I knew the next step was a ventilator, but I was doing everything I could not to get bad enough to need that, as I heard it was very hard to get off it.

People were sending me all types of encouragement. My nephew sent me a card talking about perseverance. Perseverance is not a long race. It is many short races one after another. That hit exactly how I was feeling - I was in a race every day. I needed to accept I couldn't just win one day. I was going to have to run a race every day. My friend sent me a prayer:

"God, be your strength in your weakness;

the hope in your doubt;

the comfort in your strength."

I knew right then that I needed to put my troubles in God's hands as I had to believe in his grace. My condition was out of my hands and in his capable hands. Another friend sent me a text: BELIEVE IN HOPE! Hope knows your heart, hope remembers the happy times, and hope loves your fighting spirit. Believe in hope. This helped me turn my fear into hope. Having hope and faith that I could weather this illness was so important in my healing.

On Thursday night, March 11, visiting hours were coming to an end. Courtney had just left, and I was praying in my room. I received a text to look out my door. My sister Karen was standing at the window looking in. She had just finished visiting with Mom, and she couldn't help but swing by my room. She wasn't allowed in, but it gave both of us excitement just to see each other. We texted back and forth for a few minutes. A nurse opened the door, and it took everything Karen had not to come in after her, but she knew she couldn't. It had to be heartbreaking for my family to have two members of our very close family in ICU at the same time. Karen left that night, not knowing that it would be the last time she would see me for a very long time.

By Friday night, March 12, my vital signs had taken a turn for the worse. My nurse came into my room and said he remembered seeing me at Sacred Heart Church because he was a member there, too. He asked if I wanted our priests called in to do Anointing of the Sick, as he saw how downhill my vitals were going. I remember my first reaction was confusion because I somehow thought I was stable. I then came to my senses and agreed I did want that. They called Tom around 5 am Saturday and told him he needed to come in as they needed to decide to put me on a ventilator. Tom got there about the same time that Monsignor Lyons arrived.

We had a very sacred time as I got the sacrament, Anointing of the Sick. I remember feeling a warm glow around me as I was getting anointed; it gave me comfort and strength. I feel strongly that the Holy Spirit embraced me at that point and prepared me to fight my battle, the battle of my life. Tom and I had time to talk before I was sedated. It was very emotional. We knew this was a big moment in our lives. What do you say to someone you love so deeply and may never see again? What do you say to the last person you may ever talk to on this earth? We were both scared but somehow, we didn't say goodbyes, as we felt it wasn't the end. I asked him to tell the kids how much I loved them. They are my life.

I didn't want the grandkids to forget me. We talked about how much we loved each other and how good our life had been to that point. I told him to know that if it was in my power, I would come back to him. He said he'd hold me to that! They were the last words that I said to Tom before they put me under sedation and attached me to the ventilator. Tom was able to see me for a few minutes after they put me on the ventilator. He said it was hard to see me with all the tubes and machines hooked up to me, but he knew it was what I needed to keep me alive.

Hours after I was put on the ventilator, my vital signs continued to decline. My pulmonary team started working with other facilities to look for a hospital better equipped to take care of my needs. They found an opening at a regional trauma center half an hour away from our home. After 12 days in the local hospital, the decision was made to airlift me to a regional hospital where they had better equipment and whose staff had experience dealing with more serious cases of COVID-19 pneumonia.

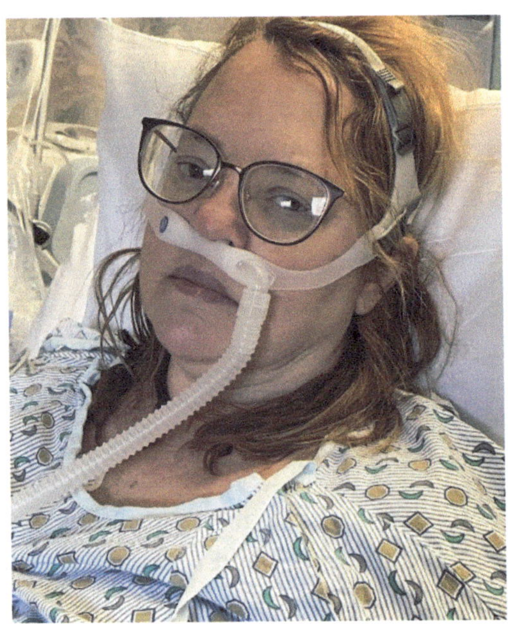

CHAPTER 5
LOSING A LIVING ANGEL

Have you ever heard the phrase "angel on Earth"? The definition I found when I looked up that phrase was someone so caring and affectionate that just being around them feels like bliss. Other characteristics were someone who puts other's needs ahead of their own, a person with a gentle soul, spreads kindness or just makes the world a brighter and happier place. In the bible, it says that God uses his angels as messengers to send warnings or to comfort or guide people through life. What a blessing to have someone in your life who shares these traits. Life is tough, so having an angel in your life is what you need to carry you through during times of need.

I arrived at the regional hospital by helicopter around 6 pm on March 13, 2021. I was told it was not a good ride for me as I was unstable the entire trip and needed 100% ventilator support. The hospital staff immediately called the ECMO team to start assessing whether I was a candidate for this treatment or not. My family immediately started to research what ECMO was to prepare for what I could undergo.

ECMO stands for Extra Corporeal Membrane Oxygenation, which is a machine that is used for patients in severe respiratory distress. The machine is better than a ventilator because it supports the heart and the lungs. The ECMO machine stabilizes patients to allow their bodies more time to fight the virus. ECMO works by inserting a plastic tube into a large vein or artery through the neck, chest or groin. This tube allows the blood to flow out into an oxygenator or artificial lung. The oxygenator adds oxygen and removes carbon dioxide from the blood before a pump sends the blood back into the patient through a separate tube at the same frequency and force as the heart. ECMO helps by acting as the patient's heart and lungs. ECMO is used when all other medical options have been exhausted for patients whose lungs can't provide enough oxygen to their body or rid themselves of carbon dioxide. Before COVID-19, this hospital used ECMO for about 30 patients a year. With the onset of COVID-19, they have tripled their use of ECMO and treated more than 100 patients a year in 2021. They even took the lifesaving step of borrowing ECMO pumps from other health systems to treat critically ill patients. I was definitely lucky to have ended up in this facility using this machine to battle the virus!

I was put in a prone position while still on the ventilator, sedated and paralyzed. For the next two days, I was stabilizing, and the doctors did not find it necessary to put me on ECMO, as, again, they were using this as a last resort. After their initial assessment, they found I had a fungal infection, which they started treating.

While I had been transitioning to the regional trauma hospital, my mom was still in intensive care at our local hospital. She was tolerating the ventilator very well. Her blood pressure was low due to her declining kidney issues. On March 16, Mom was having a great day. Doctors were decreasing her sedation. Her kidney numbers were improving, and she was neurologically stable. The respiratory therapists and doctors were literally ecstatic with how she handled the challenge of the ventilator.

Two days after I arrived at the regional hospital, they put a central line in me and decided it was time to place me on ECMO. The doctor called Tom to get his consent and to make sure he understood the treatment and risks, which he accepted. The daily chest x-ray showed no improvement in the double pneumonia but no worsening, which was hopefully a sign the virus was plateauing. I was hypothermic, so they placed a Bair Hugger on me to help control my body temperature. They continued to use this to control my body temperature as needed.

The next day, I was put under anestesia for a bronchoscopy. Bronchoscopy is a procedure where a doctor puts a scope down your throat and looks at your lungs. They cleared all of the secretions and mucus out of my lungs while down there. In the next couple of days, the staff started decreasing my ECMO from 100% to 90%. This was a sign of hope that my lungs were starting to heal. A big complication of ECMO is the risk of infection. They needed to limit the amount of people I was exposed to so as to not pick up any further illnesses. I was not allowed to have any visitors at this point.

Tom's first week of not being able to see me was extremely hard. He spent much of his week withdrawing from the world under the covers in our bedroom. The reality of the severity of this horrible COVID-19 virus was setting in for him. He was getting calls from our kids, friends and family asking how he was doing and asking what they could do to help, but they couldn't help with what he needed most - me to get better and come back to him.

Tom met with the hospital's crisis counselor team of Amy and Gabby. They discussed that we had been married for 26 years. He told them we had three kids together, my son, Luke, from a previous relationship; his daughter, Megan, from a previous relationship; and our daughter, Courtney, we had together. We also had four grandkids. They talked about where we worked. He said that I enjoyed playing cards and described me as a very family-oriented person. He also said I was very happy-go-lucky and described me as his voice of reasoning. His goal, at that point, was for me to pull through this acute illness and return back home to him.

My sister, Sue, continued sending daily emails to a growing number of well-wishers wanting updates on my condition. She also started adding Mom's condition to the emails as well. On March 18, she communicated to all that Mom had improved enough to be taken off the ventilator! The nurses said it was a miracle. They never thought an 86-year-old woman with underlying conditions and COVID would come off a ventilator, but mom is no ordinary lady and definitely not ready to leave this world!

Unfortunately, the next day, Mom's condition worsened as her kidney numbers declined. They were considering dialysis if they didn't see improvement. She had a FaceTime call with my brothers, Ed and Andy, and she enjoyed every minute of it. I may talk a lot about my three sisters, but we all knew the boys hold a special place in Mom's heart! Mom was a farmer's daughter and grew up on a farm, and both my brothers picked up that love as well. She would always say she had no favorites and that she loved us all the same.

On March 20, the doctors took me off all blood pressure medication as my blood pressure had stabilized. The hospital was looking into changing the visitor policy to allow Tom to come visit one time a week. They lowered my sedation to see how I would tolerate it and see if less sedation would help my breathing. I was still on the ventilator set at 30%. I started opening my eyes as the sedation was lowered. The doctors checked my neurological stability. I blinked my eyes and looked around the room at the doctors, which satisfied the doctors. They did a chest x-ray and it showed I was improving.

That same day, Mom started kidney dialysis. She was in good spirits. Her oxygen requirements were still high but she tolerated it well. They had to put high-flow oxygen on Mom every night because her oxygen saturation went low. They continued to wean the oxygen back. She was more awake and aware of her surroundings. She commented about how loud it was in the room - she was referring to the HEPA filtering machine that was also in my room as well. She was having problems swallowing. They had to give her two units of blood because her iron was low. As expected, she was confused about how many days she had been in the hospital and why she was so weak. She worried she wouldn't have the strength to do the therapy needed to recover. She started having physical and speech therapy and started to eat small amounts of food with her pills.

There was a Catholic priest who was visiting me weekly. He administered anointing of the sick and prayers for healing with each visit.

The chaplain and counselor continued to call Tom once a week to check in on him. Tom was wondering when he would be able to at least have a visit so he could hold my hand once more. He did feel that I was getting better, but he knew there was a long road ahead of him, and he needed that visit. The counseling team got to work on helping make this happen for Tom.

On March 23, Sue emailed everyone that Mom was feeling okay and was stable. Her dialysis had to be stopped early because her blood pressure dropped too low. The doctors were talking about putting a feeding tube in the next day as they were fighting an uphill battle with the extra fluid she had in her body. My sisters, Karen and Sue, both visited her that day and said her numbers looked good and they had nice visits with her.

On March 24, Karen visited Mom in the morning and had a good visit. Sue was scheduled to have the evening visit. Mom was peacefully sleeping at 4:45 pm when Sue arrived, so she didn't wake her. Sue checked with the nurses to see how Mom was doing. The nurses stated they had just inserted a nasogastric tube in Mom in order to be able to give Mom nutrition through the tube, and they had just gotten Mom settled and wanted her to rest for a while. After allowing her to rest, the plan was to start the nutrition feeding which was sitting next to mom's bed. Suc walked around the room for a while, looking at the beautiful cards that literally covered every wall of her hospital room while Mom was resting. She frequently walked over to Mom to make sure she was okay and watched her vital signs. Mom had so many people who loved and supported her. Sue turned around and saw on the monitor that Mom's heart rate was falling, but Mom seemed to be still peacefully breathing. She went over to her bed and held her hand, confused about why her heart rate was falling and what was happening. At that time, the nurses and doctor came rushing into the room, and Sue asked them what was happening. They said, *"Your mother is dying."* Within a few minutes, her heart rate fell to zero, and she passed away peacefully without a struggle. Sue held her hand and told her how much we all loved her and told her it was time for her to go to heaven to be with Dad. The family knew mom was very sick with COVID-19, but no one was prepared to lose her so suddenly. She was the heart of our family.

My siblings and I were blessed with the most wonderful mother. She certainly knew how much she was loved by all. She was so pleasant right up until the end of her life. She did look up to the ceiling two days before she died and said, “Dori, just open the door”. Dori was her older sister, who had passed away a year before her mom. It was at that time that our family realized that Mom might not win this battle. In the words of our brother Ed: “We are sad but content that now her suffering is over. I sit here feeling the joy of understanding what the good Lord wanted for her in life and being surrounded by all the treasured ones who have been waiting for her”. We all knew that Mom was in heaven. She had no more struggles and had been reunited with our dad, Elmer, as well as her family and friends, who welcomed her into her new home.

The next few days were filled with the family getting funeral arrangements together for Mom. She had already pre-arranged many wishes with the funeral director years ago, making it easier for our family when the time came. Because of COVID, the family decided to scale back opportunities for big groups. For the viewing, visitation times were separated for groups to visit to limit the amount of people in the funeral home at one time. They collected many pictures of a life filled with family and loved to share them at the viewing. Since I was in the hospital, they had a picture of me and a sign stating where I was and how I was doing so mourners knew ahead of time before greeting the family. Tom said every time he looked at the picture, he had to walk away because it was just too hard to look at. It was very hard for my family to mourn Mom, knowing I was in the hospital, sedated, fighting for my life, and not aware that Mom had passed away. At the viewing, my friend Theresa, who is a nurse at the hospital I was in, came to give her condolences and gave Tom the news he was waiting for - he could now come up to see me once a week. This was great news in a week of sorrow.

At the funeral, my oldest brother, Ed, delivered a riveting eulogy. Below is a small snippet from the speech which perfectly presents the essence of our mom:

To many, mom's house felt like a home should feel like. It was a place where the word welcomes on a doormat extended through the front door. She had an open-door policy, and at any time, we would find her talking with our friends who were waiting for us. She would offer her home and her good food and they would leave with a hug and kisses from her with an invitation to come again. She had a way of making you feel so special with her undivided attention and optimistic banter. When asked how she made her congeniality look so effortless, she gave credit to watching her mom and dad interact while raising a family of 13 kids and running a farm.

After delivering his prepared speech, Ed turned to mom's casket in the church and, off the cuff, gave a big request to our mother. He said, "Mother dear, since you are so close, be brave and ask God for his indulgence for our sister Julie to expedite her way back to us. Ask him to find the love in his heart to keep her with us and let her have the twilight years that he allowed you to have with us."

CHAPTER 6
PRAYER WARRIORS ASSEMBLE

Prayer has always been an integral part of my life, ingrained in me by my faith-filled family. My uncle was a Catholic priest, and I have two aunts who are Sisters of Christian Charity. Growing up, family gatherings often included mass or shared moments of prayer. My mother frequently recounted the story of her large farming family, with thirteen children, coming together every night to pray the rosary in their living room.

I also attended 12 years of Catholic school, where I learned that prayer is our means of communication with God. Yet, how often do we find ourselves asking for something from God but not receiving it? This can lead to doubt about the effectiveness of prayer. Some may view prayer as a simple "ask and you shall receive" practice, but is it truly that effortless? Perhaps we have received what we asked for but didn't recognize it because it manifested differently than we expected.

Prayer goes beyond simply requesting things from God. It allows us to worship and praise the Lord privately, confess wrongdoings and seek forgiveness. And yes, it is a means of asking for things that we truly desire for ourselves or loved ones. But how many are willing to submit their will to God and have faith that He knows what is best for us? Confirmation that God has heard our prayers may come in the form of a peaceful and calm feeling after praying. Prayer is a powerful tool that opens up a personal space for us to connect with God on a deeper level.

A prayer warrior pledges to pray for others selflessly and wholeheartedly. It is a precious and meaningful gift to offer someone. My prayer warrior team initially consisted of my closest friends and family, but as word spread about my hospitalization, it grew to include extended friends, coworkers, community members, classmates, and even strangers. With each new addition, our group grew stronger and more vigorous in its prayers. Sue's daily email updates were forwarded to an increasing number of individuals, resulting in an ever-expanding network of dedicated prayer warriors.

The following month tested the patience and faith of my family and friends. After 17 agonizing days, Tom was finally able to see me at the regional hospital on March 30th. My lifelong friend and hospital employee, Theresa, greeted him at the entrance and escorted him to the ECMO unit. She knew it would be difficult for him to witness what he was about to see. Once inside the unit, Tom saw a doctor already in my room, who acknowledged him and asked if he was comfortable with seeing blood. Tom assured him that he was. The doctor then offered for Tom to observe the trach insertion procedure, which he eagerly agreed to. Despite the overwhelming sight of me in such a condition, it proved to be therapeutic for Tom to finally be able to see me in person and hold my hand. He noted that I appeared swollen but had good color, and he cherished the hour spent with me.

Tom felt a strong support system from our family and friends during this trying time. He received numerous meals and gift cards for food and gas and began visiting his sister Gina and her husband Billy for dinner on a regular basis. They provided him with home-cooked meals and listened to his daily struggles. Our children also checked in on him regularly through phone calls.

The staff at the ECMO unit were exceptional in their care for me. They were proactive in addressing any issues that arose, such as my elevated heart rate prompting a CT scan, which revealed a Staph and yeast infection, both of which were promptly treated. Unfortunately, I sustained injuries during my hospital stay, including a laceration above my eye from a monitoring device, swelling and subsequent loss of part of my tongue from biting down on it, an enlarged spleen, another UTI, and required multiple bronchoscopies to clear my airways. A PEG tube was also inserted for feeding purposes, allowing crushed medication to be administered directly into my stomach.

Tom's days were filled with loneliness, spending most of his time on the back porch praying and watching our dog Logan roam. His sister Gina sent him two prayers that gave him comfort, which he recited daily by himself and with me whenever I was able to see him. He also led these prayers when together with my family.

SERENITY PRAYER:

God, grant me the serenity to accept the things I cannot change,

courage to change the things I can

and the wisdom to know the difference.

HEALING PRAYER:

In our minds, body and souls,

wherever our pain or disease may reside,

May it be released within the white lights of the Holy Spirit.

Tom felt inspired by the multitude of prayer warriors who were devoutly saying the rosary for him every day. He was determined to do the same but encountered two obstacles: he didn't have a rosary and couldn't remember the prayers. He reached out to Karen, hoping to borrow a rosary from her. By chance, the previous day, Karen had stopped by our mother's house and found an envelope addressed to her from Our Lady of Fatima. Inside was a stunning rosary. Karen attempted to say the rosary herself but couldn't recall the correct order of the prayers. The next day, Tom called Karen in search of a rosary. At that moment, it dawned on Karen that the rosary was not meant for her but rather for Tom. She happily gave it to him as a gift from above. Now equipped with a rosary, Tom needed to learn how to properly pray it. He planned on looking up instructions online, but something remarkable happened instead. While observing his dog Logan playing outside, Tom noticed Logan chewing on something and went over to investigate. To his amazement, he discovered a booklet on how to say the rosary! Tom was filled with awe at these incredible occurrences and knew they could not simply be dismissed as coincidences; they were undoubtedly acts of divine intervention.

The initial weeks of April were uneventful. However, the emergence of acral ischemia, or digital necrosis, on my extremities alerted the doctors to a lack of circulation in those areas. Gradually, my fingers and toes turned red and developed a black covering due to reduced blood flow caused by ECMO treatment for my heart and lungs. The nurses diligently measured the extent of discoloration on my digits as an indication of its rapid progression. Despite Tom's weekly visits, he could not escape noticing the steady spread of the condition on my fingers, toes, and feet.

Tom continued to attend his crisis counseling sessions, where he discussed the overwhelming amount of support he was receiving from both family and friends during this challenging time. He shared that his adult children were eagerly anticipating their mother's return home, and they were all committed to supporting her throughout her recovery. When asked how they could assist, Tom expressed a desire for more frequent updates from the doctors rather than just the nurses. He also expressed gratitude for the spiritual counseling calls he had been receiving.

April 4th, *Easter Sunday* - A day typically spent with family, filled with joyous egg hunts and church services. But for me, it was a day of constant monitoring, blood tests every four hours, and fervent prayers for a miracle. In Sue's email that morning, she mentioned my love for Easter and how I always looked forward to indulging in chocolate. So my sister asked everyone to pray and enjoy some chocolate in my honor. Tom made a visit with his family that day. His sister, Angie, organized an egg hunt for her grandchildren, bringing some light into an otherwise heavy day.

On days when Tom could be there, he would read me the e-cards sent by friends and family. The nurses took on this task on other days. They also went above and beyond to care for us. They would braid my hair to keep it healthy and out of the way, and they kept Tom updated on any new developments. It amazes me that these individuals took the time to care for someone they didn't even know while juggling numerous pressing tasks during each shift. To me, it speaks volumes about their compassionate nature as caregivers. Tom always assured me that I was in good hands when he couldn't be there, as the ECMO staff were all exceptional in their roles.

Throughout April, I experienced multiple days of stable health. Tom would often reassure me by saying, "No news is good news." Under the care of my doctors, my body was complying with their expectations and allowing the machines to do their work. As the days passed, my usage percentage of ECMO decreased significantly: from 80% on April 18 to 70% on the 21st, and finally down to 60% on April 24. This marked a major milestone in my recovery process. However, amidst all this progress, my family was struggling with the fact that it had been one month since my mother's passing, and I was still unaware. They were grappling with how to break the news to me once I woke up and became more stable. It was important to them that I hear it from them personally rather than through social media or a text message. Meanwhile, discussions about what to do with my mother's house and belongings had already begun, but they wanted to involve me in the decision-making process as our family has always done things together.

In the midst of my hospitalization, a zoom meeting was organized by the nurses on April 25 for my family. My kids, sisters, brothers, and Tom gathered at my sister Karen's house and filled her living room. It had been a while since anyone, aside from Tom, had seen me since I moved to the regional hospital. As soon as they saw my face on the screen, the room fell silent. Seeing someone you love hooked up to so many machines with trachs and IVs can silence even the most talkative Smith family! While I was sedated and paralyzed, Tom sat on the floor by the computer and talked to me.

After getting over the initial shock, everyone took turns singing songs, talking to me, comforting each other, and praying together. I'm sure my parents were there in spirit as well, praying for my recovery and providing comfort to our family during this emotional journey.

On April 26, my feeding tube was changed to a G-J tube in order to help with some intestinal issues I was experiencing. Towards the end of April, the staff noticed that my blood pressure was dropping significantly at night. Despite this, they were able to stabilize it each time. An echocardiogram revealed that the right side of my heart was not functioning properly. To help control my blood pressure, they started me on a medication called Flolan and inserted a Swan Ganz catheter through my jugular vein to measure pulmonary artery pressure in my heart.

On Tuesday, April 27, Tom came to visit as usual. He followed his routine of donning a gown, speaking with the nurses, checking all of my vital signs, talking to me, saying prayers, rubbing my legs and holding my hands (which he always said were cold!). But this day was different - as he finished his prayers and opened his eyes, he saw that mine were open for the first time. He squeezed my hand, and I was able to squeeze back. When he moved to the other side of the bed, I followed him with my eyes. It was a small victory for Tom, as it was the first sign that I might be aware of his presence.

That night, Tom posted an update on Facebook about his visit. He expressed his joy that I seemed to be "coming back" and thanked everyone for their love and support during this difficult time for our family.

CHAPTER 7
A PLUNGE ON THE COVID COASTER

Close your eyes and remember your first roller coaster ride. The fear of the unknown was overwhelming, mixed with anxiety and uncertainty. You stepped onto the ride, fumbling to secure the safety harnesses multiple times. The announcement for departure made it clear that there was no turning back now. Your mind prepared for the climb as the cart clicked up the first hill. Adrenaline rushing, you had to remind yourself to breathe. At the top, you handed over control to the ride operator or maybe even the universe itself. Holding onto someone's hand for support, you braced for the plunge down the first hill. Just when you thought you survived, the cart raced around in a spiral, building up speed again. Panic set in, and doubts flooded your mind. But before you could think about it, it was already time for the next drop. A gut-wrenching scream escaped your lips, a new level of emotion you never knew before. Closing your eyes only made it worse, so you quickly reopened them. Some may have cried or even passed out during this part - it was all too much to handle. Numbness took over as the ride continued through loops, spirals, and tunnels until finally coming to a stop. You made it! After gathering your thoughts, a new feeling emerged - one that left you conflicted on whether to ever go on a ride again or run back in line. As you stumbled off the ride, talking excitedly with friends about your experience, you realized it was something you'd never forget.

This reflection only scratched the surface of what living with a chronic illness felt like for both the patient and their loved ones. It was a rollercoaster of emotions - from anticipation to fear, anxiety to occasional moments of excitement. Every decision was second-guessed, and the future seemed uncertain in the face of this illness. You had to trust strangers with your well-being, hoping they knew what they were doing. And while you did everything in your power to help yourself, doubts would creep in about whether it was enough. Panic, screams, and desperate prayers became a regular part of the journey.

On April 29th, my physician assistant was just putting her coat and lunch bag down for the day when she heard the rapid response team call to my room for a cardiac arrest. She rushed to my bedside and found my blood pressure had plummeted to 40 over 20. Without hesitation, she began chest compressions to restore blood and oxygen throughout my body while the rest of the rapid response team arrived. Simultaneously, the Catholic priest was called to my room. Although he couldn't enter, he prayed in the hallway and, in his words, threw blessings into the room and prayed for me. After some stressful moments, the team was able to stabilize me. They did a CAT scan of my chest, abdomen and pelvis, revealing a pocket of fluid in my lungs. They started me on Lasix to help drain fluid and increased ECMO back to 100% to allow the heart and lungs to rest. Tom was called into the hospital and came up to spend some unplanned time with me that day. After leaving, he sought solace with his sister Gina and her friend Trish, who provided much-needed emotional support. The COVID coaster was in full throttle. Despite the grim prognosis, Sue's email that night hinted that it was a bad day, but in the spirit of positivity, she just continued asking for extra prayers. My friends and family were so full of fear that I would be among the statistics of people who did not survive, yet all refused to believe what seemed to be inevitable.

Slowly but surely, as my vital signs began to strengthen, the medical team cautiously lowered the ECMO settings. Flolan, a powerful medication used to treat pulmonary artery hypertension, was proving to be effective. However, during a routine bronchoscopy later in the week, the doctor made a startling discovery: my right lung was battling a fungal infection, and my left lung had been invaded by yeast. In response, they had no choice but to crank up the ECMO to 100% once again in order to give my body time to rest and fight off the infections. It felt like one step forward, two steps back.

Despite these setbacks, there was some glimmer of hope. A few weeks ago, when I first arrived at the regional hospital, I could barely manage to hold 20 millilitres of air in my lungs during a breathing test. But now, after six weeks of intense treatment and care, that number had increased to 200. While still far from the average person's capacity of 500 millilitres, it was a sign that I was making progress in the right direction. Even with all the obstacles thrown in my way, I refused to give up. The rollercoaster ride of ups and downs continued on, but I held onto that small piece of hope with everything I had.

The next hurdle came as a nurse discovered something dark and ominous in my ECMO line. The nurse immediately contacted Tom, her voice heavy with concern for the day ahead. She explained that this could be a grave situation - if the spot was yeast, there was hope for treatment with medication, but if it was fungus, the outcome could be deadly. The waiting game began as they sent off samples to be analyzed, knowing it could take days for results to come back. Tom pressed for more information - how would they know which infection it was, and how would they treat it? The doctor's answer was grim - they would have to use powerful antibiotics to aggressively fight against whatever was lurking in my body. They were pulling out all the stops, determined to save me. Every tube and line were changed, and every precaution was taken to eradicate any trace of infection. It was a race against time, and my fate hung in the balance.

Coincidentally, my sister Sue had just started working at the same hospital I was in and happened to be training at the same hospital where I lay fighting for my life. Tom called her to share the latest setback - another potential threat to my recovery. As she stepped into the hallway to take his call, she bumped into my doctor, who was searching for a pathologist to review the findings in my ECMO tube. Without hesitation, she introduced herself as my sister and informed him that she was aware of the situation. With her guidance, he found the right doctor to discuss treatment options. It felt like angels were guiding us throughout this journey, directing doctors and staff towards the answers we desperately needed.

A few days passed, and they found a blood clot in the ECMO line. It's much better to find it in the tubing where they could clear the blood clot out rather than have the clot get into my system. Just another example of how good the medical team was being proactive and on top of their game! Changing out ECMO tubing is not an easy task, but the skilled team did what they needed to do to keep me safe.

The journey had reached another milestone day - Mother's Day. Our normal routine that day was for the kids to come over for breakfast. In the afternoon, we'd visit Tom's mom and spend time with her and the evening would be spent with my mom. Ironically, this year, it was most likely my mother showering blessings from heaven on me to help in my recovery. There was a strong consensus amongst my family that she gave up her battle on this earth to go to heaven and help Dad gather a team from above to help me recover. What a glorious thought! At 4 o'clock that day, the nurses arranged a Zoom meeting with my kids and grandkids. Tom had the kids gathered at our house for the meeting. There were tears as soon as my face came on the screen as it was the first time some of the family had seen me. With the way they had my hair done up that day, I looked exactly like my youngest daughter, Courtney, which freaked a few family members out. I was still sedated, so I was not aware of the meeting. They again took turns talking to me, even though I was not able to respond. My youngest grandchild walked into the room and said, "Grandma looks dead", and ran off - just some comic relief for an overwhelming situation. What a hard thing for my kids to see on Mother's Day. I always did my best to shield my kids from trauma of any magnitude, but they needed to stand tall and face reality, which they did with amazing strength.

As the week progressed, I received more blood transfusions. I started coughing up food with each feeding tube release. I was having problems with sedation. My heart rate increased to 140. Tom came into my room on his scheduled day that week, and the nurses had the healing music channel on the TV. He went about his routine of kneeling by my bed and praying. He was going through a ton of emotions and was crying. The nurse came in because there was an alarm going off as one of my IV bags was empty. Through tears running down his cheeks, Tom said, "Can you please show me how to change the station? The music is breaking my heart. Also, I know my wife would not like it so can we get better music on?" The nurse showed Tom where the music was, so after that day, Tom had full control of my music in the room. There were some days he would come in, and the country was playing, and he told the nurses that I didn't like country, so please don't expose her to that or elevator music - 80s rock was perfect!

Tom was always supportive and respectful to the staff taking care of me. On National Nurses Day, Tom left my room for the day and approached the nurse's station. He thanked all the staff for all they were doing to help me and all the patients they were helping. He saw all the work they were doing on a daily basis and felt they deserved praise.

Tom continued to get calls from crisis counselors and the chaplain. Tom voiced his appreciation for all that the team was doing. He was receiving updated information and felt like he had a good understanding of the situation. He admitted to worrying about me. He just wanted to "get through this and move on". Some days were better than others, and he was being strong for our children. His faith was strong and he knew the good Lord had things in hand even if we didn't understand. He held to the idea that each day was a gift and that tomorrow was not promised for any of us. His hope was that I would get through this and be able to move on with life. He did understand that life may look very different on the other end of this illness. He also understood that there was the possibility that things wouldn't "get better". Tom saw that he had become stronger through this process and that whatever happened, the course of his life had changed. He didn't want to live life without me but knew that he would be able to do what he needed to do.

May 15 - the day of my sister Karen's 60th birthday. This was a day I'm sure I would have been sending her some silly old lady balloons and flowers or celebrating with a trip to the casino, but unfortunately, I was not even aware the day was special. Instead, I was dealing with secretions coming from my trach site. The foul smell suggested infection again. My nephew and her husband threw a nice party for Karen to celebrate. The family enjoyed celebrating the milestone, but when it came to taking pictures, it was difficult for them to take our traditional '4 sisters' picture we take at almost every outing without me there. I've been told these celebrations were very hard for my family emotionally, as they felt an emptiness of mom not being here to celebrate with them, as well as me being in the hospital for so long. They tried hard to celebrate the many birthdays and holidays the best they could.

The doctors were still monitoring the necrosis on my limbs. They started to put nitroglycerin paste on my fingers and toes. They hoped that would help with circulation and stop the growth of the necrosis. They were still concerned about my blood pressure issues. An echocardiogram showed my heart was sounding better, although they were still seeing tachycardia. My blood pressure started dropping, specifically overnight again, going as long as 80/40. The last few weeks have been full of critical moments.

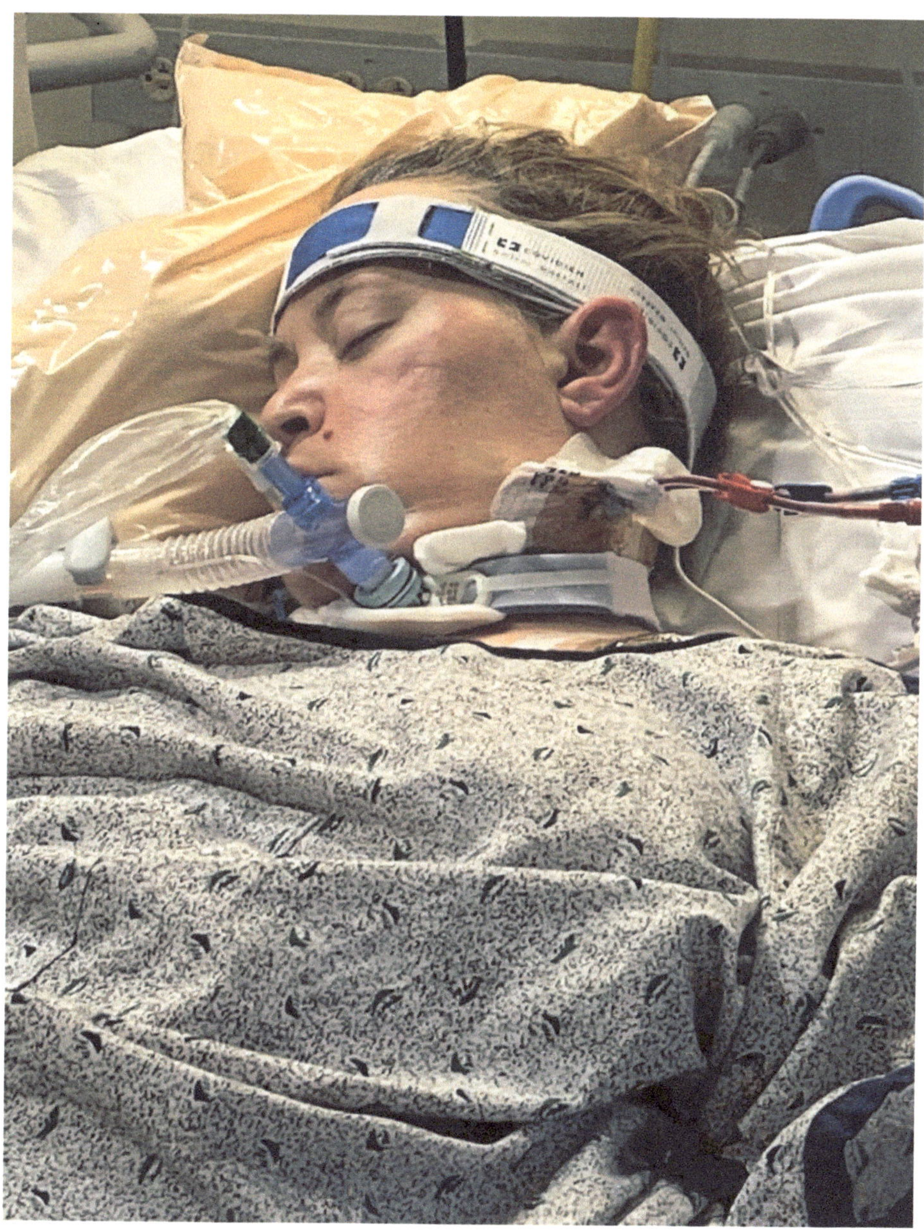

CHAPTER 8
HAVING HOPE UNTIL THERE IS NO MORE HOPE TO BE HAD

What is HOPE, truly? The dictionary defines it as the desire for something to happen or be true. It embodies wishful thinking, creating a sense of anticipation for something positive on the horizon. In the Old Testament of the Bible, hope is more than just a wish - it is a deep trust and patient expectation. It is a belief that what is hoped for will come to pass without doubt or fear.

In the New Testament, we are reminded that Christ was sent to us to bear the weight of our sins and to provide for all our needs, both now and for eternity. Hope, then, is not just a fleeting feeling but a foundation of faith that sustains us through trials and tribulations.

The act of hoping shapes our character, as it requires patience and perseverance in the face of uncertainty. It illuminates the darkness of despair, offering a glimmer of light and a belief that things will ultimately work out for the best. Hope transforms our perspective, allowing us to see beyond the present moment and envision a brighter future.

In times of struggle and adversity, hope is a beacon of strength that guides us through the storm. It is a powerful force that empowers us to face whatever challenges come our way. Hope is not just a fleeting emotion - it is a lifeline that carries us through the darkest of times.

On Tuesday, May 18th, Tom made his usual visit. He engaged in a lengthy discussion with my pulmonary doctor, seeking to comprehend the rationale behind the decision to increase the ventilator settings while decreasing the ECMO settings. The doctor explained that they were striving to strike a delicate balance between the two machines that would prove most beneficial for me.

Later that evening, a sudden deterioration in my vital signs occurred. My heart rate soared to 140, and my blood pressure read 100/50, yet the doctor deemed me stable. It was discovered that I had developed enterococcus or lactic acid bacteria in my system, prompting an urgent CAT scan at 10:00 pm. During the scan, my oxygen levels plummeted to a harrowing 60%, necessitating immediate intervention to stabilize me. However, I struggled to tolerate lying flat on the bed, resulting in a distressing drop in oxygen levels to a perilous 40%, causing my skin to take on a ghastly purple hue.

As the medical team deliberated on palliative care options, my prognosis grew increasingly grim. Throughout the night, I battled worsening septic shock, lactic acidosis, hepatic renal failure, and deteriorating respiratory function. A comprehensive CT scan was conducted on my head, chest, abdomen, and pelvis, revealing the extent of the challenges I faced.

Early that morning, the rapid response team was once again summoned to my room due to a dangerous drop in my blood pressure. Chest compressions were administered to elevate my blood pressure, unfortunately resulting in a broken rib. Following stabilization, a series of tests revealed a bloodstream infection and declining kidney function. Kidney dialysis was initiated to address fluid retention, while the ECMO and ventilator were adjusted to 100%. The medical team informed Tom that I had regressed to a critical condition, marking a significant setback. I was also placed back on Flolan to support my heart function.

The nurses promptly contacted Tom and provided him with an update on my condition. Upon receiving the call, Tom immediately made his way to the hospital. As he entered the room, he was struck by the chaotic scene reminiscent of a MASH surgical room, with blood splatters from chest tubes and used medical supplies scattered across the floor. The nurse informed Tom that they had attempted to clean up some of the mess, but not all of it, before his arrival.

Concerned about the severity of the situation, Tom inquired with the doctors about the possibility of calling the patient's family to say their goodbyes. After assessing the monitors and observing the patient's condition, the doctor reassured Tom that there was still time before taking such a drastic step. The patient's quick rebound and stabilization were seen as positive signs by the medical team.

One positive development from that day was the approval for Tom to visit me daily. The staff recognized the positive impact of Tom's visits on my well-being. Tom consistently maintained a positive attitude and was well-received by all staff members, making his daily presence a welcomed addition.

Following the second code, the medical team reconvened to discuss my condition with Tom. The topic of palliative care has been broached several times in recent weeks, given the extended duration of my ECMO treatment. The doctors inquired about Tom's level of optimism regarding my recovery. Tom's unwavering response was that he "had hope until there was no more hope to be had. Until my heart stopped beating and stayed stopped, he had hope". Tom's steadfast commitment to my well-being was truly inspiring. It was as if his positivity and determination were somehow transferred to me subconsciously. Such a resolute belief in the face of a dire illness was undeniably powerful.

The next day, I experienced an atrial fibrillation episode. A CAT scan was done to check for blood clots. Tom visited me that day and was shocked by my swollen appearance due to fluid retention from kidney issues. My eyes were bulging to the point that they were opened, and Tom dropped to his knees and broke down in tears when he saw me. While the nurse comforted him, Tom asked her how sick I actually was, at which she informed him that I was the sickest patient in the hospital, which was significant for a regional trauma center. Tom had a difficult time seeing me in such a state but gained a better understanding of my condition after speaking with the doctor.

Tom spoke of how much of an emotional roller coaster this whole process had been for him and the rest of the family. He understood the situation with his head, but his heart was not wanting to acknowledge the truth. The family and our entire prayer warrior group kept praying for the best outcome.

Doctors continued daily efforts to improve my condition, including chest tube insertions to clear the fluid in my lungs, more bronchoscopies and blood transfusions to get my blood counts back up. They started proning me again in hopes of clear secretions from my lungs. They were able to take ECMO down to 70%. They continued to lower my sedation to do testing and when they did it towards the end of May, I started coughing, which was a good sign my lungs were healing. I ended the month of May with ECMO set at 50%.

As I entered the third month of my hospital stay, the doctors expressed concern that I had reached a plateau in my recovery. Despite being on 60% ECMO for nearly a week, any attempts to reduce the percentage resulted in a drop in my oxygen levels, necessitating an increase in the machine's settings. A CAT scan revealed that my left lung was slowly healing, while a gelatin layer on my right lung was impeding the recovery process. A procedure was performed to remove the gelatin layer, but it proved to be too thick for suction. The medical team decided to proceed with a VATS procedure the following day. VATS, or Video Assisted Thoracic Surgery, involves making an incision in the chest to examine the lungs with a scope and remove the gelatin layer through a separate incision.

Numerous masses were organized across the country with the specific intention of praying for my recovery. Churches such as Annunciation Church, Immaculate Heart of Mary, and St. Joseph all held masses in the past week, with prayer intentions focused on my health. My devoted family, cousins, and friends attended these masses, joining different congregations and religious groups in prayer for my well-being. Additionally, my aunt, a Sister of Christian Charity, enlisted the help of many sisters worldwide to pray for me daily. The collective hope was for a successful surgery that week. It was truly remarkable to witness the outpouring of support from individuals who were complete strangers to me yet took the time to pray for my recovery and inquire about my progress.

The following day, the decision was made to postpone the procedure until Friday, when their top thoracic surgeon would be available to perform the operation. The plan was to conduct a thoracoscopy with pulmonary decortication, a procedure aimed at cleaning out the right lung and removing a layer of gelatin material that was hindering lung expansion. Despite previous discussions between my pulmonologist and the surgeon regarding the procedure, the surgeon ultimately deemed the damage to my lungs too severe for a successful surgery at that time. The timing was crucial for the procedure to be effective.

Throughout this challenging time, Tom remained my primary source of support and communication. He skillfully balanced the information he received from medical professionals with his unwavering belief in positivity, which he sought to convey to me and those inquiring about my condition. Tom consulted with Sue daily to determine the content of email updates, carefully selecting information to maintain a sense of hope and optimism among recipients. His guiding principle was, "We accept the bad days, and we celebrate the good days."

Tom came into the room to visit the day before my surgery. The nurses were brushing my teeth. I was trying to move my head around to see him, but he told me to wait until they were done. When the nurses were done, and he came around to look at me, he told me how beautiful I was, as he always does, and then paused and said, I hope you still think I look good too. I nodded my head yes. Then the nurse was holding one hand, and Tom was holding the other hand, and the nurse asked me to squeeze both of their hands and I did without hesitation. This was an encouraging sign I was very stable going into the procedure the next day, which was great!

The procedure was successfully performed on June 4th, although there were some delays in the operating room, which caused the surgery to start late and last longer than anticipated. This understandably left many anxious individuals waiting for updates that evening. Fortunately, Tom received a call at 9:30 pm confirming that the surgery went well and was tolerated "like a champ". The surgeon was able to remove all the gelatin material from the right lung, resulting in an impressive 85% lung capacity post-surgery. The doctor did mention that there may be a temporary setback in the days following the surgery as the body recovered, but significant improvements should be seen shortly thereafter. Additionally, one liter of blood was administered that night to aid in the recovery process. Three tubes were inserted into the right lung to drain any oozing resulting from the lung scraping. In the words of the surgeon, there is a high level of confidence that the patient will soon be able to be removed from ECMO and the ventilator.

The next day was a positive one. When Tom entered the room, the nurses and doctors greeted him with smiles, expressing their happiness for our family. This medical team had become like family to Tom, witnessing his struggles over the months. They had been there for him through every step of progress and setback, sharing in his joy at my improvement.

Within two days of the surgery, the ECMO machine was gradually reduced to zero support. They were only circulating my blood through the machine without adding oxygen to test if I could maintain stable numbers without ECMO assistance. Tom had a wonderful visit that day. When he walked in, I opened my eyes wide and smiled, a sight he hadn't seen since my hospitalization in March. I tried to speak to him, but he reminded me of the trach tube preventing me from talking. I gestured for a kiss, and he obliged by blowing me one from a distance. Unsatisfied, I motioned for him to come closer and give me a real kiss on the lips, which he did. I then silently expressed my gratitude, mouthing, "I couldn't have done this without you."

We continued to communicate through gestures, with Tom asking questions and me nodding yes or no. The nurses provided Tom with a book containing pictures and questions to aid in our communication. Tom found this form of interaction uplifting, describing me as his voice of reason. Not having me to talk to for so many months had taken a toll on him.

Since March, Tom had been collecting all the mail we received and piling it up. He felt it disrespectful to look through mail addressed to me, which is sweet, but not exactly practical. He knew I paid all the bills online and assumed they were getting auto-paid through the bank. I always paid the bills, so he didn't know how to access the online banking account. He also didn't know what I had set up to pay automatically and what I didn't. In June, he discovered notices from the bank, gas company, and internet service that we were past due and services would be terminated if we didn't address the bills. Determined to resolve the issue, he called the bank, learned how to use online banking, and successfully paid all the bills, restoring our services. This was a significant accomplishment for him, as he had never managed bills or used online banking before.

A week after my surgery, I began retaining too much CO2 while still on ECMO. A new medication was administered to stabilize my blood pressure, which tended to drop when I fell asleep. Despite my inability to speak, I had a FaceTime call with Courtney during Tom's visit. Though communication was challenging, I found solace in seeing Courtney on the screen and hearing her voice, which brought me comfort.

On June 14th, after enduring 91 days of challenges, a major milestone was achieved. Tom entered the room and looked at our favorite ECMO tech, Lance, who asked him if he had said anything different in the room. Tom said he saw it as soon as he walked in – I had been taken off ECMO, and the equipment had been removed from the room. This moment marked a significant victory for both Tom and the ECMO team, who had worked tirelessly to reach this point. Witnessing the success of seeing other patients struggle with ECMO must have been a rewarding experience for both Tom and the dedicated medical team.

I was gradually becoming more alert each day and engaging with the nurses. They would ask me questions, and I would respond with nods. One day, they inquired about my music preferences, and when they mentioned rock music, I lit up with a smile and nodded enthusiastically. They played rock and roll music for me, and I thoroughly enjoyed it. I even found myself tapping my foot to the beat. The nurse cranked up the volume, and we had a little jam session.

My health was improving as I strung together good days without needing kidney dialysis. My vital signs were stable, and my oxygen levels were excellent. The sedation was gradually reduced, and an ultrasound confirmed no blood clots. They even got me out of bed and onto a recliner to help wake up my muscles.

The following day, they lowered my sedation further, and I started showing signs of agitation, which was expected after being heavily sedated for so long. I had a heartwarming FaceTime call with my sisters during Tom's visit. They encouraged me, expressed their love, and shared how the whole town was rooting for me.

As I spoke with more family members, I learned about the strength they found in their faith during this challenging time. Tom, during a humbling moment sitting on the back porch of our home, prayed for guidance and told God he was handing his worries over to him because he had given all he had. At that moment, he felt a profound sense of peace wash over him and a feeling that everything would be okay. Acknowledging one's limitations and surrendering to a higher power during times of hardship can lead to profound moments of grace and reassurance. Tom's encounter with the Holy Spirit brought him solace and renewed hope, shaping his perspective on my recovery journey.

As COVID cases decreased, the hospital updated its visiting policy to allow two support people. Courtney was scheduled to visit the next day, marking an exciting moment after 97 days of separation. On June 17th, significant progress was made in my recovery journey. I was taken off the main sedation medication and had a reduced dosage of the second sedative. A CAT scan confirmed no bleeding from the lung surgery, addressing concerns about falling hemoglobin levels. Despite soreness at the ECMO site, pain management was in place.

The highlight of the day was that Courtney finally got to see me! Courtney came to the hospital with Tom. She remembers looking around the room and seeing two towers filled with IV medicines, which was overwhelming. Although I was very tired and slept most of her visit, it was a great day for both of us.

The following day, all three chest tubes were removed as lung drainage ceased, and a chest x-ray indicated continued improvement. When Tom arrived at the hospital that day, he Facetimed with my sister Sue. She noted just seeing the expressions on my face, especially my smile, and seeing me focus was so relieving. She said the "old Julie" was back and had a lot to say, although I was talking too fast and no one could understand what I was saying! The doctor reinserted the kidney dialysis catheter as a precaution. Tom marveled at my progress without ECMO and dialysis, praising the care team and expressing faith in my recovery.

My first memories post-coma involved conversations with Tom. To me, it felt like I had just woken up from the day I was put on the ventilator. I had no memory of the whole ECMO experience. I remember asking Tom what happened, and he said, "You have no idea what you've been through!". I just couldn't believe I lost three months of my life sleeping! I remember Tom telling me how beautiful I was and that I had the strength to win this battle.

On June 21, I was transitioned to a step-down unit from intensive care, signaling a positive step in my recovery. I was completely off sedation but experienced agitation as my body adjusted. Despite being unable to swallow, I persistently tried to call the nurse for water, showcasing my determination and spirit. Tom's unwavering support and patience were instrumental in navigating this challenging phase. He tracked down a nurse and got some swabs to relive the dryness in my mouth, but not before he and the nurse had a good laugh at my feisty spirit to get what I wanted.

CHAPTER 9
A TIME TO HEAL

Healing is a challenging journey, filled with ups and downs, setbacks, and small victories. Survivors of long ICU stays face various issues like post-ICU syndrome, PTSD, depression, delirium, anxiety, and drug withdrawal. The healing process involves physical and emotional recovery, with sleep being crucial but often disrupted for ICU patients. It's important to take things one step at a time, prioritize self-care, and acknowledge the pain as part of the healing process. Putting oneself first is essential for healing.

After spending 101 days in a regional hospital, I was transferred to a long-term rehab hospital in York. During the transfer, I was given medication to relax, which made me sleep through most of my first day at the new hospital. That gave Tom time to speak to the doctors about my medical journey. The new doctors were hopeful for a full recovery despite potential long-term effects of ECMO and COVID. Adjusting to my new surroundings and understanding the severity of my illness was challenging. I continually asked Tom to go over what all I had been through and still could not quite comprehend it.

The new hospital allowed two visitors per day, providing more opportunities for family and friends to visit. Tom brought Luke up as my first visitor there, his first time seeing me since hospitalization. They experienced my agitation from medication withdrawal, as I constantly kept pushing the button for the nurse, but they just reassured me of my progress and strength.

My sister, Karen, visited the next day. Despite my speech difficulties, Karen understood me well, which isn't surprising because we have a way of knowing what each other is thinking by just looking at each other! Even without speaking, I found joy in being part of the interaction and shared a smile at a funny comment Tom had made.

In the following days, my sisters, Sue and Lori, and my daughter, Megan, visited me in the hospital, bringing flowers, cards, and gifts. Their presence made me realize the extent of the support and prayers I had received. During Lori's visit, I mentioned seeing children playing at the end of my bed, even though there were none present. This was one of the first instances of me experiencing such visions.

Shortly after being transferred to the rehab hospital, I encountered setbacks due to infections. I developed a fever, low blood pressure, and back pain, leading to the discovery of a Staph infection in my bloodstream. These complications hindered my recovery progress.

On June 27th, it was my mother's birthday, the first since her passing. Our family deeply felt her absence, but we believed she was watching over us and aiding in my recovery journey.

The respiratory team began the process of weaning me from the ventilator, which was challenging due to the prolonged use of the machine. The relationship with my respiratory therapist was crucial during this time as they helped me breathe comfortably and guided me through the weaning process. Some team members were more empathetic, while others pushed me to progress quickly, causing anxiety. It quickly became a love/hate relationship for me!

Tom met with doctors and respiratory teams during each visit and became an expert on what numbers to monitor to gauge my recovery. Physical therapy sessions focused on rebuilding my muscle strength, starting with simple stretching exercises. After just a few sessions, they had me sitting on the side of the bed (with a lot of assistance!). The staff quickly caught on to how much of a fighter I was.

I experienced nausea and stomach issues, leading to the prescription of Protonix and consultation with a GI doctor. Blood transfusions were scheduled to address low hemoglobin levels. Ventilator weaning progressed from pressure support to using a trach collar, a process of placing a collar over the breathing tube of the tracheostomy and blowing humidified air. I started out with 4 hours and would continue increasing as I could tolerate.

Communication with visitors improved, and I showed signs of responsiveness. Nausea persisted, possibly due to antibiotics, hindering the weaning process. A stomach X-ray confirmed the feeding tube's correct placement, and Zofran was used to manage nausea. Zofran quickly became a word that every nurse could understand me saying, as I said it every time they came in!

By July 5th, I was weaning for 1 hour and 45 minutes with Tom's support. The staff found it beneficial to conduct ventilator weaning during Tom's visits as he helped settle me and keep me focused. Tom would fan me with whatever he could find in the room to cool me down and then cover me with blankets when I got cold. This back-and-forth continued throughout the weaning process. The respiratory team appreciated Tom's dedication to ensuring my comfort during this challenging time, which helped distract me from my breathing issues and allowed me to wean for longer periods. When I was alone, I struggled with anxiety attacks and had to stop the process. The nurses and respiratory techs couldn't provide the same level of attention as Tom, leading me to give up on weaning at times. It's remarkable how a little distraction and tender loving care can boost mental resilience.

By the second week of July, I could tolerate about 3-4 hours of weaning per day. Despite feeling tired and experiencing an elevated heart rate, the respiratory therapist was pleased with my progress. They likened the weaning process to exercising my lungs, emphasizing the need to gradually build up endurance. Nausea from medication persisted, but my visitors noticed a significant improvement in my alertness and ability to engage in conversations. We shared moments of prayer during each visit, which brought a sense of calmness. Both mentally and physically, I was making strides and growing stronger with each passing day. The weaning process gradually increased as my tolerance improved.

Tom's daily visits in the afternoon provided me with much-needed support. One day in mid-July, I surprised him by revealing that I could talk. The respiratory therapist confirmed this by fitting me with a speaking valve, allowing me to communicate with Tom. It took some effort and guidance from the respiratory team, but I managed to utter a few words, including "I love you," which deeply touched Tom. He recorded a video message for my family, friends, and prayer warriors, expressing gratitude for their support and love. Another video was dedicated to my children and grandchildren, where I sent them love and blew them a kiss. Tom shared these videos with our family and on Facebook, evoking emotions and amazement at hearing my voice again.

In July, I made progress by gradually increasing my time on the trach collar to 13 and a half hours. My nausea medication was changed, and I started feeling better. My daughter Megan visited me, showing me pictures of my grandkids, especially her daughter Violet, who had grown a lot since I last saw her. Tom brought me an iPad, set up by Courtney's husband, Kenny, to watch movies and videos. Despite my tremors and necrosis affecting my fingers, I was determined to use the iPad. Kenny got me a stylus pen to help.

The many days of weaning were improving my lung capacity, reaching 400 ml. My visitors were continuing to distract me and make hospital life tolerable. Tom jumped in my bed with me when I was cold, making us both smile. After one of Courtney's visits, she set up the iPad for me to watch "A Star Is Born." If I had a voice, I'm sure I would have been singing along with the songs!

Tom continued advocating for me, questioning the staff about my weaning process and ensuring my needs were met. Transitioning from a top-notch ECMO ICU team to a long-term rehab center does present challenges, as the level of care and attention is just not comparable.

The urinary catheter was removed, and we were able to test out my bladder function. One less tube and one more working organ! Luke visited and showed me videos of the kids swimming, bringing joy to my day. Seeing glimpses of my kids and grandkids having fun in the summer was great to see but also hard to comprehend at times because it was still winter the last time I stepped foot outside. After Luke left, I Facetimed Tom on my own for the first time - another milestone.

My ventilator weaning increased to 18 hours a day, with two hours on the trach collar. I was breathing with just oxygen support, a significant improvement. I sent Tom a message about my progress and asked him to have a good night's sleep because I was having a good night. He Facetimed me, and I answered – another first. This week marked several rapid improvements in my recovery journey.

I cherished the quality time I spent with each of my visitors. Growing up in a large family, it was rare to have personal conversations as most talks were in groups. How often do you get a chance to have a two-hour heart-to-heart with a family member or friend? Despite my inability to speak, I found solace in listening to my visitors express themselves. Each visit became a precious memory for me, as the visitors had time to express things to me they may not have said in the past because I would interrupt with my talking. This also extended to interactions with the staff, where I had the opportunity to observe and learn from simply listening, a skill I wasn't always adept at in the past.

By July 18th, I had progressed to 21 hours of weaning, primarily on pressure support with some trach collar weaning. The respiratory therapists commended my determination to liberate myself from the ventilator. They emphasized the uniqueness of each patient's journey, making it impossible to predict when I would be completely weaned off the ventilator. They likened the weaning process to climbing a hill, where my lungs and muscles needed to regain strength after relying on the ventilator. Considering my physical limitations pre-COVID, the uphill battle of weaning was a challenge I never anticipated.

Physical therapy has yielded significant progress. Just a week prior, I struggled to move my hand, but now I could lift it enough to remove my glasses. This milestone was achieved through consistent practice. With improvements in both physical mobility and breathing, Tom and the staff began discussing the next steps in my recovery journey. Tom researched local facilities and their admission criteria, identifying a suitable option for my continued rehabilitation. They initiated discussions with a highly-rated inpatient rehab, monitoring my progress closely. While Tom remained cautious about looking too far ahead, ensuring I received the appropriate care in the right facility was a top priority for him.in

During the weaning trials, I continued to struggle with anxiety. It was challenging to remain calm while experiencing difficulty breathing and becoming more aware of my situation. Tom was always supportive and helped distract me during his visits. Talking with my second visitor of the day also helped take my mind off things. Despite these efforts, I still required additional support, so the medical team prescribed medication for anxiety and depression. Lorazepam or Ativan were the medications initially used to address my anxiety.

On July 20th, Day 141, in the hospital, I experienced breathing difficulties again. My oxygen levels had been low for the past two days, preventing me from participating in weaning trials. The respiratory therapist adjusted the ventilator back to 40% while they investigated the issue. A CAT scan of my lungs was ordered, with results expected the following day. Tom visited during the day, and Karen visited at night. Karen noticed that I seemed preoccupied during her visit, smiling and looking around the room. When she asked what I was looking at, I mentioned seeing angels all around. I described them as beautiful and asked Karen to make room for them by moving back. I was visibly at peace with the presence of these angels in the room. Eventually, I asked Karen to leave so the angels had enough space, even though her visit wasn't over. I explained to Karen that these angels were there to watch over and protect me. Karen, sensing my comfort with the situation, bid me goodbye and left, feeling emotional about the experience. She stopped by the nurse's station and asked them to keep an extra close eye on me that night because of what she had just experienced.

After each family visit, feedback was shared with Tom and Sue, who then decided what to include in the nightly email update sent out by Sue. My sisters also had a nightly FaceTime call to discuss the day's events. The day in question was particularly emotional as they tried to make sense of the 'angels' incident. Was it a hallucination, or were there truly spiritual beings present? The uncertainty surrounding that night's events added to the stress experienced by my loved ones throughout this journey.

Following Karen's departure, I had an uneventful night, but the next morning, I was unresponsive when the nurses tried to wake me. It was discovered that my CO2 levels were elevated due to fluid in my lungs, making it difficult for me to breathe properly. Ventilator settings were adjusted, and I was given Lasix to address the fluid buildup. Tom arrived at the hospital around 1:00 pm and helped me understand the situation, calming me down. Despite his presence, I still experienced episodes of confusion, prompting a head CT scan, which came back normal. A procedure to drain fluid from my lungs was scheduled for the following day. A lung CT scan revealed deterioration since my transfer to Memorial Hospital.

Luke met up with Tom in the parking lot that afternoon and learned about my condition. Upon entering my room, Luke observed me in a confused state, talking rapidly to someone and expressing a desire to go to heaven. Although I had moments of clarity recognizing Luke, I would quickly revert to conversing with unseen individuals. Luke left with a heavy heart, sensing it might be the last time he saw me. The nurses' expressions as he departed confirmed his apprehensions. Later that night, Lori visited Luke's house to discuss his visit, and they were joined by other family members for ice cream. During their gathering, Sue received a surprising FaceTime call from me. The grandkids eagerly wanted to speak with me, and the phone was passed around so I could see everyone enjoying their ice cream. Everyone marveled at my alertness and ability to operate the phone. The doctors explained to Tom that my condition was typical of COVID, with fluctuating good and bad days, sometimes within the same day. It was another instance of the unpredictable "COVID coaster" in action.

On July 22nd, the doctor completed an ultrasound-guided thoracentesis, drawing only 10 ml of dark, red fluid with clots from my lungs. This was only about one teaspoon and nowhere close to the amount that was in my lungs. They next step was to put a chest tube in, but Tom reminded the doctors that they attempted to do that in York, and the secretions were just too thick to come out through a chest tube. Tom requested a second opinion before going any further. The second doctor took a look at the notes and requested a CAT scan with contrast be done to see if the gelatin layer had reformed on my lungs. They were scheduling that to be done in the next few days. I had no physical therapy the past few days due to my confusion and weakness. I started to have tremors again, which was frustrating because I couldn't use my phone or iPad again.

One of my first dreams (or hallucinations) that I remember was of mom and dad sitting on a park bench. Dad had his arm around Mom, and they were enjoying the peace and beauty of nature. I walked up to them and asked if I could sit next to mom. She smiled at me and said, "It's not your time to be here yet." She said that space was saved for someone else. Mom never denied me anything, so I should have found this suspicious!

My eldest brother, Ed, visited me on the 144th day of my hospitalization, and I was thrilled to see him. Despite being 12 years older than me, we share a similar mindset and have a strong bond. Ed has a knack for uplifting others and highlighting the positive aspects of life. He gave me a motivational speech, expressing his confidence that I could overcome COVID. Sometimes, a push from your older sibling is just what you need! We prayed the rosary together, and although he struggled to read my lips during our conversation, his presence was comforting. After the visit, he went to Karen's house to unwind. It must have been tough for him to witness his sister's battle and feel helpless, except for offering prayers.

The next day, both Tom and Sue came to discuss the incident involving high CO2 levels, but I had no recollection of it when they inquired. Sometimes, the mind and body shield you from memories that are best forgotten. The family continued to update a growing number of people through daily email chains, with hundreds eagerly awaiting news of my condition and offering prayers. During Tom's visit that day, I shared the dream where I saw my parents. As my mental clarity improved, I started asking more about my mother to various visitors. Most believed I wasn't ready to hear the news of her passing, so they reassured me that she was doing well, which, in a way, wasn't entirely untrue. Tom understood the need to address the topic with the family.

On July 25th, the second opinion doctor visited me to review my medical records. After assessing my current tests, he decided against another CAT scan and planned to consult his colleagues before outlining the next steps. My daughter-in-law, Natalie, who was a hairdresser, visited me and took care of my hair, which had become tangled and unkempt during my hospital stay. The hospital's grooming standards were not as meticulous as the previous one, so Natalie's efforts to detangle my hair and improve my appearance were greatly appreciated. It was a delightful experience to be pampered by her as we chatted, laughed, shared stories about the grandkids, and prayed the rosary together.

My daughter, Megan, also came to visit that week. We looked through recent pictures of Violet, and I asked Megan about my mom's condition. I expressed my concern that I wasn't getting the full picture. Megan, like others, shared the information with Tom, hinting that I should be informed soon.

I had another dream about my mom. She kept showing up at different family gathering, but she would show up alone and sit quietly and watch us. When we would notice her and ask where she came from, she said the train brought her to see us. She said she was currently living in a town outside of heaven's gates. There was a waiting line to get into heaven, and until it was her time to go in, she had to live in this town. She could see dad inside the gates; and he was dressed in a suit of gold and was sitting with a group of "big wigs" around a table. She was worried that when she got inside heaven, Dad wouldn't want to be with her because she was just a lowly housekeeper, and he was now something big. We assured her he would still love her. When it was time for her to leave, she reached into a golden purse she brought with her and pulled out a ticket to get back to her town. We walked her back to the graveyard and saw a golden train fly by, and she disappeared into it.

When Tom visited the hospital the next day, I shared the dream I had about my mom's passing. He asked if I wanted to know the truth, and I said yes. Tom then revealed that my mom had passed away in March. Surprisingly, I took the news calmly, almost as if I had already sensed it. Sue visited that night, and we discussed my mom's service and her final days. Additional prayers were requested from the prayer warriors to help me cope with the news and find peace.

My doctor deemed the lung surgery too risky and opted against it. After a week's break, I resumed the weaning process and was off the ventilator for 5 hours. The nurses noticed increased coughing, attributed to mucus breaking up in my lungs, a positive sign. Tom's pep talk reassured me that I could overcome this challenge. The opportunity arose for my close friends to join the rotation of visitors who came to see me. My long-time friends Melissa, Jen, Tracy, Julie and Theresa all took turns lifting my spirits and spending quality time with me. I also received a treat when my brother Andy and his daughter Jocelyn, who lives on the west coast, came to visit. Not all of these visitors came on good days, but their prayers, positive words and their presence truly helped in my recovery.

In late July, I resumed physical therapy sessions, progressing from sitting on the bed for 45 minutes to standing the next day, marking the first time in 150 days that I put weight on my feet. The therapist also washed my hair, a simple act that brought immense comfort. The goal was to improve mobility and boost my morale for the healing process.

The first week of August presented challenges as I struggled with weaning off the ventilator. Lori and Tom noticed changes in my behavior, including more hallucinations and talking too fast to understand. Tom would come in and ask what I watched on TV that day. I was watching The Olympics or Golden Girls, or other things I never watched before and he would laugh. A urinary tract infection and pneumonia were diagnosed, leading to antibiotic treatment and nebulizer therapy to aid breathing.

Hallucinations persisted, with vivid visions of military soldiers protecting me in my room. They were dressed in old-style dark green uniforms, and they were carrying weapons, but they weren't threatening to me, as I knew they were there to protect me. Despite the surreal experiences, I found comfort in their presence. As I battled through infections, the infectious disease doctor ensured I received the right treatment. By the end of the week, I felt better and resumed physical therapy and ventilator weaning.

On August 5, I communicated mouth sores to Tom and the nurses, a significant milestone as it was the first time I wrote legibly on a whiteboard. A visit from my brother Ed brought solace as we prayed together, drawing inspiration from biblical stories of healing and support during tough times. He mentioned stories of Lazarus and Simon carrying the cross for Jesus. He explained to me that when the burden is hard, God will appoint someone to help you get through the tough times.

While I focused on recovery, my family prepared for an estate auction at my mom's house, evoking memories of our shared past. The separation during this process added to my grief, highlighting the emotional toll of my hospital stay.

During this period, lucid dreams blurred the lines between reality and imagination, causing confusion upon waking. I inadvertently texted friends in my sleep, reflecting dream scenarios in my conscious actions. I'd be confused as to why Tom was visiting me when he had just been tortured by someone the night before or he left me for another woman. When I tried to explain to him my confusion, it was just too hard to convey, so I would get frustrated and let it go.

Amidst my recovery, Tom faced additional stress as his mother was hospitalized, requiring ventilator support. The strain of caring two loved ones' health weighed heavily on him, underscoring the challenges of this period. Sue's email added Ellen, Tom's mother, to the prayer list for the ever-growing prayer warrior group.

Hallucinations persisted, leading to misunderstandings about my son's well-being and unfounded concerns about my daughter's marriage. The line between dreams and reality blurred, causing distress and confusion. Despite the support around me, I grappled with emotional turmoil and doubts, a common struggle in illness.

Despite having a ton of family, a great medical staff, a waiting list of visitors to come visit me and cards and messages to lift my spirits each day, I fell into a dark place. I would cry most days Tom came to visit. I cried when the nurses would come in to take care of me, and I couldn't be of assistance to help with my basic needs. I was not sleeping well, and everything felt like more than I could handle. My dreams had me doubting my relationships, my worth, my family's health, and my safety in the hospital - all things that were just not true, but my dreams and thoughts were deceiving me. It doesn't matter if you have an army around you or if you are alone; the darkness and demons come knocking. It's a reality of sickness. I finally started distinguishing dreams from reality by figuring out if what happened was in the hospital room or other places. I knew I wasn't mobile and I wasn't leaving my room, so anything happening that wasn't inside the hospital room had to be a dream. This helped me start seeing the fault in my thoughts and seeing the good everyone was doing for me.

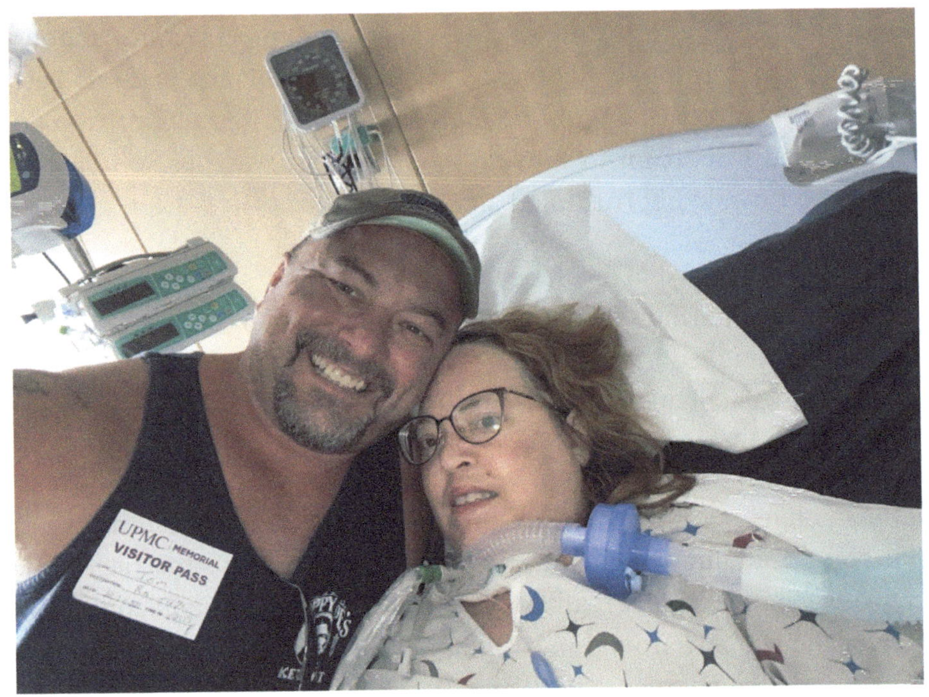

CHAPTER 10
PNEUMONIA 2.0

As my condition was deteriorating at the long -term rehab facility, Tom was working with multiple hospitals trying to have me transferred. Most hospitals were at (or over) capacity, so unless they saw a case they could turn around quickly, they weren't inclined to accept a patient that had a long-term treatment need. However, the right information got to the right people at the regional hospital where I had received ECMO treatment, and I was accepted back to their facility to treat my pneumonia. My family was incredibly pleased with the care I received there a few weeks ago, so this was a welcomed move. The only downside of this transfer was the visitor policy returning to only 1one person as a visitor, which would be Tom.

The 53 days that I spent at the long-term rehab hospital definitely had their ups and downs. Weaning from the ventilator went well, but many infections caused setbacks. The quality of care was not up to par and my family had to advocate too often for better care. The staff would apologize and tell us they were understaffed or they were with other patients, but when it happens every day, and it affects your recovery, it can't be tolerated. I am forever grateful my family stood up and became my advocate. While they were fighting for me to get the best care possible, I was swirling in my own world of hallucinations and bad dreams, presumably brought on by months of sedation and the anxiety medication I was currently taking! After both hospitals completed the transfer requests, they promptly sent me by ambulance back to the regional hospital to treat the newest pneumonia.

Part of my new assessment testing was a CT scan of my lungs. The doctors said all my other body organs were working well, but there was extreme damage in my lungs from the COVID-19 pneumonia. I had fluid in both lungs with scarring fibrosis. The doctor referred to my condition as end-stage lung disease, and again, the discussion of palliative care was being considered. After examining my extremities, the doctor noted they would eventually need to do some amputations of my toes. They also noted I had a large sore on the back of my head that hadn't been treated at the last hospital. They had their wound team come in and start treating this wound. Some of my hair was shaved to get to the wound to clean it well. My hair was not well taken care of at the previous hospital, and I had large knots that needed to be cleaned and worked through. In addition, clumps had been falling out, and general thinning was happening, a common side effect many COVID patients were experiencing.

There was a happy surprise for my sisters when I initiated a group text to my sisters asking them how the estate sale for Mom and Dad's house went over the weekend. This was an active text group for years that we would blow up talking about everything but was silent for the past few months. How great to have it start up again with a text from me!

Struggles with anxiety and hallucinations continued, even with the change of hospitals. I explained to the nurse that I was trying not to take Ativan because we thought it was adding to my anxiety. When she came into the room the next time, I told her I had a fear of being tied to the bed, and I didn't want to fall asleep because of that. I also asked her why the cops were at the hospital. She said they weren't and did what she could to calm me down. She gave me a bath and tried to brush my hair, but it was too matted. I finally agreed to take Ativan because I needed to relax. The balance between reality and my dreams and hallucinations was a daily battle for me, but I don't know how much of that my family or medical team knew. The next day, I continued to have hallucinations. I thought there were dogs at my feet. I didn't believe I was in bed, even though I was. I told everyone to get out of the room, even though there was only one nurse in the room. That night, I saw a cat in the room. During therapy, I thought there were other people in the room, and I was talking to them enough that they couldn't continue therapy. The doctors started Xanax and switched the Ativan to Lexapro to help with the hallucinations and anxiety.

A team of pulmonologists at the hospital convened to discuss my case and concluded that a double lung transplant was the best course of action due to the severe condition of my lungs. The right lung was particularly affected by the COVID virus, with the doctor describing it as "destroyed." Both lungs showed signs of damage, including fluid and fibrosis. To improve my breathing, a chest tube was to be inserted into the right lung to drain excess fluid, and I was receiving lasix to help remove fluid from my lungs. The pulmonologists were in contact with John Hopkins and Temple University to explore the possibility of transferring me to their transplant programs. Despite the poor state of my lungs, my oxygen saturation levels were in the mid-90s, the ventilator was set at 50, and I was able to take in 400 to 450 milliliters of air, which was considered positive.

My cousin, Helen, gifted Tom a prayer shawl crafted by the parish council of Catholic women at St. Joseph's. Each stitch in the shawl was accompanied by a prayer. Along with the shawl, a card featuring a picture of Mother Teresa and a heartfelt prayer was sent. Tom had the hospital staff drape the shawl over me after a procedure to extract fluid from my lungs, during which a chest tube was inserted.

On August 19th, I had a productive physical therapy session where the therapists noted a significant reduction in my anxiety and commended my cooperation. They were assisting me in relearning basic self-care tasks like washing my face. Tom joined in the session and made it enjoyable by participating in exercises with me. We even shared a light-hearted moment where I playfully threw punches at him as instructed by the therapists. Later that night, I FaceTimed Karen, who was thrilled to see my expressions and personality returning.

The doctors were still finalizing the details of the lung transplant, which involved a considerable amount of paperwork and coordination with hospitals. The prospect of undergoing such a major surgery after already spending six months in the hospital was daunting. I longed to be back home with my family in my own bed. The idea of facing a complex surgery like an organ transplant while still recovering mentally and physically overwhelmed me.

Through daily physical therapy sessions, I made progress in being able to sit on the side of the bed for 40 minutes within the following week. My therapist was pleased with my core strength. Tom's visit that day was positive, allowing us to engage in deeper conversations, including discussing my mother's passing. I expressed acceptance of her death and my readiness for the lung transplant, believing that there was much life ahead of me and a strong desire to return to normalcy.

Tom noticed the absence of my usual scent at home and missed it. He brought my favorite Bath & Body scented soap and lotion from home for my next bath, which brought a sense of familiarity and comfort. My medical staff commented that I had the best smelling room in the hospital! As time progressed, I established a connection with the nurses. One nurse developed a unique technique we called the 'Tasha Twirl' to administer medications through my tube more effectively. This technique involved swirling the medicine in the tube to combat the gas in my stomach, causing a tornado effect in the tube. The nurses provided emotional support through gestures like holding my hand during anxious moments and applying lotion to help me relax.

The monotonous hospital routine was starting to wear on me as I became more alert and conscious of my confined surroundings. Misplacing my call bell in the bed was frustrating, especially when I needed assistance and couldn't communicate verbally. It was a challenge to reach for it when my movement was limited. There had to be a more efficient way to stay organized while bedridden.

In late August, the respiratory team introduced a vibration machine to help clear the secretions in my lungs. An attachment was connected to my tubes, delivering varying levels of vibrations to break up scar tissue and mucus in my lungs. One therapist likened it to a "lung massage," though it felt far from relaxing. The treatment triggered coughing spells as I expelled excess mucus. Each visit from a respiratory therapist heightened my anxiety, hindering my progress with the therapy. Mental fortitude was crucial for my recovery.

Anxiety persisted, prompting a switch from Ativan to small doses of morphine for calming effects. This adjustment proved more effective. Periodic blood transfusions were necessary when my iron levels dropped. Tom remained a beacon of optimism, encouraging me to stay positive and have faith during challenging moments. His transformation from a hot-tempered individual to a supportive partner was remarkable.

We received an update from Temple University, our preferred choice for a lung transplant. They had all the required test results and were evaluating my case. Due to high patient volumes, the hospital was operating at full capacity and unable to accommodate as many cases as desired. The doctors assured me that they were providing regular updates to Temple. They emphasized the importance of meeting recovery milestones like weaning off the ventilator, sitting up in bed, managing anxiety, and building mental resilience to prepare for the surgery. I diligently followed their guidance, eager to undergo the procedure and return home.

I was feeling increasingly frustrated about not being able to eat or drink anything as all my nutrition was administered through my feeding tube. It was particularly challenging to see commercials showcasing delicious summer foods that I couldn't enjoy. A simple morning coffee or a piece of chocolate would have lifted my spirits immensely. The nurses cautioned against eating while on a ventilator due to the risk of aspiration, which was understandable, but I longed to savor the taste of food. Before this sickness, a chocolate frosty from Wendy's would always make me feel better on a bad day!

On the last day of August, Tom and I had a lengthy discussion with our doctor and received some encouraging news. The medical team was impressed by the progress I had made since returning to the hospital. I was visibly stronger, spending less time on the ventilator each day, and showing improved oxygen saturation levels. My anxiety was subsiding, and I was becoming more focused. The doctor mentioned the possibility of weaning off the ventilator without the need for a lung transplant if my progress continued. He attributed my recovery to my determination and eagerness to return home. Despite facing similar challenges as other patients, I maintained a positive attitude and diligently followed their instructions. The doctor shared a story of another patient who defied expectations and recovered unexpectedly, emphasizing that every patient's journey was unique.

The doctor outlined a plan to gradually wean me off the ventilator, taking into account my improved strength. The schedule involved morning weaning sessions, followed by physical and occupational therapy, and additional weaning in the late afternoon. This structured approach aimed to make the weaning process more manageable for me.

During Tom's visit the following day, I was in high spirits, listening to music and engaging in light-hearted moments with him. I was actively participating in therapy sessions and showing progress in my mobility.

On September 2nd, I spent 8 hours in a recliner chair and received a visit from three ICU nurses who had cared for me during my ECMO treatment. Their excitement at seeing my progress highlighted the impact of my journey on those who had supported me. Although I didn’t remember them, Tom did and they were able to connect on the progress they’ve seen.

The nurses devised a solution to satisfy my desire to taste liquids by using mouth swabs dipped in a mixture of apple and cranberry juice. This simple gesture brought me immense pleasure. They also introduced Mio squeeze bottles with various flavors to provide a sensory experience without the need to swallow.

September 4th marked the first Penn State game of the season, which Tom and I watched together at the hospital. It offered a welcome distraction and a reason to celebrate. I underwent a 12-hour weaning session that day, coinciding with Penn State's victory. The doctors shared promising insights about lung recovery post-COVID infection, indicating the potential for lung regeneration without the need for transplants. They praised Tom for his unwavering support and positivity throughout my journey, acknowledging his crucial role in my recovery. The therapist noted the joy I exuded whenever Tom visited, underscoring his significant impact on my well-being.

Courtney FaceTimed me that night, and I was grateful because I was in the midst of an anxiety attack. Tom was at her house, and together they managed to calm me down within 10 minutes. I had a mucus plug in my trach that was difficult to clear. After the respiratory therapist removed it, I experienced continuous coughing, which was quite frightening. These episodes occurred multiple times a day, some more severe than others, and took a toll on my mental well-being.

As Labor Day weekend approached, I couldn't help but feel a sense of loss. This weekend usually marked one of my favorite times of the year - our family reunion with my dad's side of the family. The reunion, which typically involved over 200 relatives spanning multiple generations, was a cherished tradition. It included a day filled with food, drinks, raffles, card tournaments, games, and laughter with lifelong acquaintances. As the current president of the organization, missing the event that year was heartbreaking. Fortunately, my brother Ed stepped in as acting president, ensuring the reunion went on smoothly. Despite not being physically present, I had a FaceTime call with many cousins who had been praying for me daily. It was heartwarming to see everyone, and I even won a raffle thanks to their support.

Before, not on my birthday, my favorite nurse, Amber, surprised me with balloons, flowers, and a birthday celebration with other nurses. Their gesture of love and care overwhelmed me, and I felt truly blessed by their kindness. The outpouring of support and well-wishes from the hospital staff made me realize the incredible friendships I had formed during my stay.

September 8th marked my 51st birthday, a day filled with love and surprises. Tom spent most of the day by my side, and my family arranged a card shower with an abundance of cards, gifts and lottery tickets. The thoughtful gestures, including a personalized power hour video created by my nephew Bubba. My family got together that night and watched the video together, Facetiming me to share in the fun. Despite the circumstances, I felt surrounded by love and positivity throughout the day.

A friend of Karen's gave her holy water from Lourdes which has proven to create blessings and miracles. Tom would bless me with this water daily as we said prayers together.

Shortly after my birthday, I faced a setback with an infection at my trach site, leading to a blood transfusion and antibiotic treatment. Tom's daily leg massages and prayers, along with the use of holy water, became a routine to promote healing and faith. As my condition stabilized, the doctors recommended transferring me to a long-term care hospital to continue my recovery as the hospital was again at max capacity. Temple had responded and said they wanted me to get stronger before they considered the lung transplant.

Despite initial concerns about the new hospital, we proceeded with the transfer as it was necessary for my ongoing care. The decision to focus on strengthening my condition before considering a transplant was reassuring, and we remained hopeful for a positive outcome on this challenging journey.

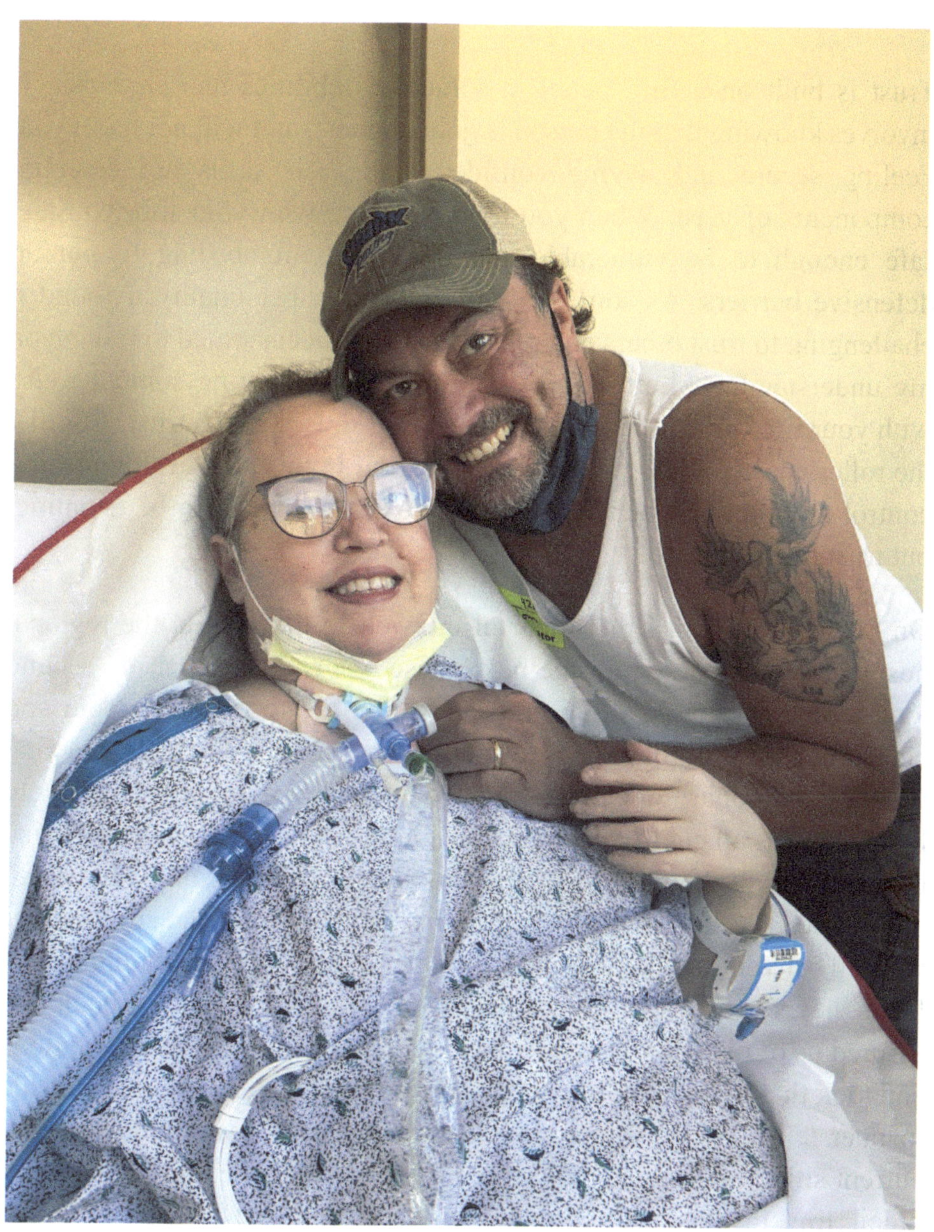

CHAPTER 11
TRUST THE PROCESS

Trust is built on a firm belief in someone's abilities and character. It involves knowing that the person is good, honest, and will not harm you. Feeling secure and having confidence in their skills are essential components of trust. When you trust someone with your life, you feel safe enough to be vulnerable and open without needing to put up defensive barriers. As someone with a Type A personality, I found it challenging to trust others completely, as I was accustomed to relying on my understanding. Letting go of control and entrusting someone else with your life can be scary, but it is only possible through trust. Just like the roller coaster analogy I mentioned earlier in this book, relinquishing control and putting your life in someone else's hands can be daunting, but trust must flourish.

On September 23rd, I bid a tearful farewell to the staff at the regional hospital as I embarked on the next phase of my journey at my second long-term rehab facility. Tom accompanied me to my new room and helped me settle in following my ambulance transfer. We had a meeting with the pulmonary doctor at the new hospital, whom we immediately liked. He was an elderly gentleman who pulled up a chair and sat beside my bed, taking the time to discuss my medical history and address all our queries. He shared stories of patients similar to me who successfully weaned off ventilators, offering a glimmer of hope. After examining my lungs, he expressed confidence that I might not require a transplant and assured us of his ability to assist me. He inquired about our expectations and took the time to familiarize himself with us. His exceptional bedside manner left a lasting impression on me, and I felt reassured about my current situation. He delved deeper into the reasons behind my frequent blood transfusions, ruling out internal bleeding. He explained that individuals with chronic illnesses like mine often experience chronic anemia, necessitating periodic transfusions until full recovery, a scenario he believed applied to me.

The hospital's visitor policy allowed for two visitors per day, which was quite exciting. Tom visited daily, and one additional person could also visit. On the first day, Courtney came to visit, and it had been two months since I last saw her, so it was a joyous reunion. Just before her arrival, a specialist permitted me to start sipping water, which was a moment of great happiness as I hadn't had a drink in nearly seven months. The drink had a blue dye, and my secretions were checked to ensure none went into my lungs. Fortunately, my swallowing function was good, and I could continue drinking water. I was so thrilled about this milestone that I asked Courtney to take a picture of me with the blue water when she arrived.

My spacious new room offered a stunning view of mountains and trees. The oversized bed could easily accommodate two people, prompting Tom and me to joke about sharing it. I appreciated the company of more visitors, including Lori, Karen, and Megan over the next three days. Their presence lifted my spirits and rekindled my optimism. Simple gestures like hugs, hand-holding, and sharing stories meant the world to me and all my visitors. Tom faithfully visited me every day, providing support, focus, and assistance with my weaning trials.

On September 24th, we celebrated our 27th wedding anniversary. Tom surprised me by bringing a picture from our wedding and hanging it on the wall in front of me. He then joined me in my oversized bed, and we spent his entire visit watching TV together. The nurses couldn't help but chuckle when they saw how thrilled we were to have this quality time on our special day. Since we had just been admitted to the hospital, they probably thought we were a bit crazy!

Because my water intake was progressing smoothly, I was permitted to have a small amount of fruit on the 27th. It was delicious, and I had no issues with chewing or swallowing, which was a positive development. Unlike many individuals with a tracheostomy for an extended period, I did not experience any swallowing difficulties.

My friend Melissa visited me and noticed a significant improvement in my appearance since she last saw me at the first rehab hospital a few months ago. During her visit, a nurse also mentioned how delightful it was to come into my room because I was always pleasant and appreciative of the care provided by the nurses. I have made progress in my self-care routine and can now independently wash my face, brush my hair, and brush my teeth.

Luke informed me that he would embark on a 72-mile running challenge in my honor starting in October. He has also invited others to join in. He mentioned that his mother's perseverance inspired him to push through despite his initial struggle with running. This was a significant challenge for him as he couldn't even run half a mile at the time. The purpose of the challenge was to show solidarity and support for me without any fundraising involved. I was deeply touched by his thoughtful gesture and felt immensely proud of him. I expressed my hope that everyone participating would stay safe. In the past, I had attempted to train for a 5K on four occasions but always faced injuries before completing the run.

On September 28th, the nutritionist increased the amount of food in my diet. I enjoyed a bite of apple with peanut butter and a few pieces of fruit. After this successful trial, I was given the green light to transition to a regular diet starting the following day. The plan was to gradually reduce the use of the feeding tube once I could consume 75% of my meals orally. This would eliminate one source of potential infection and allow another organ to function properly.

Courtney visited me again the following day. I introduced her to my new relaxation therapy - coloring in adult coloring books. I found this activity to be incredibly calming, and it helped improve my breathing by keeping me focused and reducing my anxiety. I had a book filled with inspirational quotes, and as I finished coloring the pages, I displayed them on the walls of my hospital room. This practice helped me maintain a positive mindset during challenging times when I felt alone. When my friends and family learned about my coloring hobby, they showered me with a generous supply of coloring books and various coloring tools. Their overwhelming support brought me joy and comfort.

The following day, I weaned for 12 hours. Sue paid me a visit, and upon her arrival, I was joyfully enjoying a meal of turkey, mashed potatoes, and green beans. I managed to consume about a quarter of my meal, which was a significant achievement considering I hadn't eaten in 7 months! That night, I stayed up late, engrossed in coloring. I would become so absorbed in my work that when I finally looked up from the page, 2-3 hours had passed. I transitioned from using colored pencils to markers, feeling like a child in an art class!

On September 29th, my day started early when a nurse arrived at 5 am wanting to give me a bath. In the past, I would have just gone along with it, feeling frustrated because I couldn't express my preferences. However, as I was recovering, I started advocating myself and told the nurse that I didn't want a bath at that early hour as I was still sleepy. My first shift nurse later noted this on my board to ensure I wouldn't be disturbed for a bath again. This experience marked a turning point for me as I regained control over my care and asserted my preferences.

Additionally, I received a thoughtful gift from a friend at work - a 5-pound Hershey chocolate bar. It was so heavy that I couldn't lift it myself, but Luke kindly placed it on my shelf for me to admire until I was ready to indulge. It's interesting how life changes; a decade ago, I received the same size bar as a gift and finished within a week, but now I wonder when I'll ever have the desire or capacity to consume that much chocolate again.

Nineteen individuals had committed to joining Luke in the 72-mile challenge. I was thrilled for each of them and deeply grateful for their willingness to participate on my behalf.

In October, I took my first steps with the help of physical therapists. They used a walker and a harness to support me as I stood up for the first time in 8 months. It was a brief moment, but it felt amazing to be on my feet again. This experience made me realize the hard work ahead to regain my ability to walk.

Everyone tried to remind me of how far I had come, but my perspective was slightly different from theirs. I couldn't recall all the times I had been critical or when they were worried because I was sedated. The process of recovering from a lengthy illness was still new to me. I heeded everyone's advice to take things one day at a time and one hour at a time, understanding that I could only do as much as my energy allowed. I maintained a positive attitude and made an effort to smile at everyone who entered my room, whether it was a visitor, nurse, or therapist. I was gradually able to eat about 40% of my meals, with the rest still being administered through a feeding tube, although the amount was decreasing. As I transitioned to eating more orally, my anxiety lessened, and my stomach was no longer as bloated as it had been previously.

The running challenge started on October 1st. Some chose to walk, while others opted to run, with many offering prayers of support during their activities. I was deeply moved by the dedication of those who took on this challenge to show their support for me. Luke diligently tracked his runs on his phone and sent me screenshots each night to stay accountable. It was a refreshing change to be the one cheering him on and providing encouragement during his runs. My sister, Sue, shared in an email that she had set a personal goal to walk and run. After her first day, she gained a new perspective on my struggles and found herself thinking of me when catching her breath. Unlike the runners who could pause when out of breath, I had to persevere through every moment of weaning, spending 12 to 14 hours a day on the process.

On October 4, I resumed trach collar trials. Today, I completed a record 3.5 hours, feeling exhausted when the ventilator was reconnected for pressure support weaning. The medical team plans to combine trach collar trials and pressure support weaning to reach a goal of 24 hours on the trach collar. I noticed an improvement in my mood and confidence as I progressed.

The following day, I managed to wear the trach collar for 6 hours. During physical therapy, I was able to stand up three times, holding for 10 to 35 seconds each time. Bill, my respiratory therapist, was extremely kind and knowledgeable. He had developed a close relationship with both Tom and me. Bill expressed his belief that he could successfully wean me off the ventilator without requiring a lung transplant. He had experience working with patients with similar breathing difficulties and was confident in his ability to help me progress. His optimism was motivating me to continue pushing forward.

On October 6, I spent 10 hours using the trach collar, and the following day, I increased it to 12 hours. The respiratory therapist then connected a speaking valve to my trach, which made breathing more challenging. Despite this, I managed to keep it on for 8 hours. The speaking valve enabled me to communicate, so I took the opportunity to make some unexpected phone calls, surprising my family members, who were thrilled to hear my voice after seven months. Fortunately, my voice was strong, and I had no swallowing difficulties. When the physical therapists entered the room, I startled them by speaking to them, as they were unaware of the speaking valve.

Tom recorded a video of me speaking to share on Facebook. In the video, I expressed my gratitude for the ongoing prayers, cards, lottery tickets, and gifts that everyone had sent. The outpouring of support truly touched me, and I wanted to convey how much it meant to me and how it was helping me navigate this challenging journey. The video received hundreds of comments, showing that not only did I need their support, but they were also finding faith and inspiration in my journey.

On October 9, I spent 13 and a half hours on the trach collar. The respiratory therapist would turn it off every night to allow me to rest. I was gradually increasing my food intake but became slightly dehydrated, necessitating IV fluids. The trach tube was replaced with a smaller, more comfortable one. I found the hospital conducive to better sleep and appreciated the friendly staff and the lovely view from my window. I missed being outdoors, especially during my favorite season, fall.

On October 10, Tom's mother, Ellen, was readmitted to the local hospital with pneumonia after initially recovering at a nursing home. Sue's email that evening requested all prayer warriors to keep Ellen in their thoughts and prayers.

Friends and family continued to have masses said for me at various parishes. The outpouring of support through prayers and rosaries from so many people was truly remarkable. Our community and my prayer warriors have shown exceptional kindness in supporting my recovery. My family received heartfelt notes from various faith communities, which was incredibly uplifting. It's heartwarming to see people unite in times of need.

I had more visits from my friends now that the visitation rules were less strict at the hospital. Today, my friend Tracy, whom I have known since kindergarten, and her husband Scott came to visit me. Scott had heard about my bad dreams and sleep troubles, so he brought me an authentic dream catcher to hang on my window. It was beautiful and instantly made me feel at ease. Tracy also shared a story that resonated with me. She recounted a recent hiking trip with Scott, where they tackled a steep mountain that seemed daunting to her. Scott led the way up, and Tracy followed his footsteps, feeling unsure if she could make it to the top. However, she kept moving forward, step by step, until she realized she was almost at the summit. Reflecting on this experience, Tracy compared it to my journey, facing seemingly insurmountable challenges but persevering one step at a time. She highlighted the importance of persistence and following through with what is asked, gradually making the impossible seem achievable. I am grateful to have such a supportive friend who sees my struggles in a positive light.

My seasonal allergies flared up, and I wasn't feeling well. They stopped efforts to wean from the ventilator, which made me anxious about the possibility of setbacks in my recovery from COVID. The doctor prescribed Allegra and increased my fluid intake to address dehydration. That evening, Courtney visited, but I couldn't relax and kept coughing until I vomited a large amount of mucus, which made me feel better but embarrassed in front of my daughter. Despite the incident, I managed to settle down and breathe better for the rest of the visit. Later, when I spoke to Tom, I expressed my fear of regressing. He reassured me that setbacks are normal in any journey towards a goal and encouraged me to keep moving forward, reminding me that tomorrow is a new opportunity for improvement.

In the following days, I recuperated from a sinus infection. By October 14, I felt significantly better and resumed weaning for ten and a half hours. Although I still had a persistent cough and was expelling a lot of phlegm from my lungs, I continued to work on my adult coloring books. I proudly displayed my completed artwork on the wall, creating a growing collection that visitors, including doctors and nurses, admired. My daughter and her friend gifted me a book of adult curse words to color, which provided some amusement, although I refrained from showcasing those particular pieces. A chest x-ray was conducted to monitor my lung health, revealing some haziness that was gradually clearing up.

I was feeling frustrated about missing out on so many things in life. I had been in the hospital since March, which meant I missed spring, summer, and now fall. My grandkids experienced a summer without me and are now starting a new school year. It was football season and, more importantly, Oktoberfest season – my favorite time of year for enjoying a beer. While my focus needed to be on getting better, it was hard to see these life events passing by without me. I felt restless during the weaning process and was eager to return home. Tom always supported me, reminding me of the love and pride everyone had for me urging me to keep fighting. "I can and I will" became my new mantra.

When the physical therapist came into the room the next day, I started moving my legs to the side of the bed and began getting into a sitting position on my own. I usually needed their help with sitting up, so they were pleased with my progress and determination that day.

On October 16, the doctors continued to monitor my hemoglobin numbers and ordered transfusions when they dropped below 7, which was still quite often. Additionally, a trach change was performed. I always found trach changes uncomfortable and dreaded them. The procedure was done without sedation at my bedside. Recently, I had been experiencing a lot of coughing, leading the doctors to suspect that the trach tube might have been too long and irritating my throat. They decided to replace it with a shorter tube. However, the tube replacement did not go smoothly. While the old tube was successfully removed, the respiratory therapist struggled to insert the new one. I became agitated and experienced pain during the procedure, eventually leading to an anxiety attack. Thankfully, Tom was present during the tube change and helped calm me down by holding my hands and focusing my attention on him. Despite my growing trust in the medical staff, I still struggled to maintain that trust when things didn't go as planned.

That night, I experienced more secretions than usual after the trach change. I called the respiratory therapist, Bill, to the room because I was struggling to breathe. When he arrived, he calmly reassured me by saying, "If you can talk, you can breathe." He cleared my mucus, and we shared a laugh about his comforting words. Since that day, I have often used those exact words to calm myself when I get anxious about difficulty breathing.

On October 16th, Tom's mother, Ellen, passed away at Hanover Hall. Tom, along with his sisters Angie and Gina, were able to visit and spend time with her before she peacefully passed away that night. Ellen had been battling pneumonia and other medical conditions, and the doctors had informed the family that she was unlikely to recover. Her caring nature and warm smile will be dearly missed by all who knew her.

My heart ached for Tom and his family as we struggled to cope with yet another loss. The passing of another mother was a heavy burden to bear, especially considering the recent deaths of my own mother and mother-in-law in the same year while I was also dealing with a long hospital stay. I longed to be home with my family, to grieve together, but instead, I found myself alone in my hospital room. I felt helpless as I couldn't assist in planning the funeral, gathering photos for the memorial, or reminiscing about the good times we shared as a family with Ellen. She was a kind and welcoming woman who always made me feel special, and her absence will be deeply felt. These losses have made me realize the fragility of life and the importance of cherishing every moment we have. What lessons does God want us to learn from this?

On October 19, I managed to wear the trach collar for 16 hours, my longest duration so far. My thoughts were consumed by Tom's family, and I felt saddened that I couldn't be there to mourn Ellen's passing with them. Tom reassured me that it was alright and that they all understood, keeping me close in his heart. During the funeral, my sister arranged for a FaceTime call so I could watch the service from my hospital bed. We requested the hospital staff not to disturb me for an hour.

On October 21, we laid Tom's mother, Ellen, to rest. Tom went shopping and bought a new suit to honor his mom. He sent me a photo, and he looked fantastic. It was his first time getting a full suit like that, and I was so proud of him. I wished I could have been there with him. During the service, the priest spoke about Ellen's simple life and her love for her family. Tom's sister, Angie, and his niece, Alexis, gave heartfelt eulogies, showing how much Ellen had touched the lives of many. I was able to FaceTime for the entire mass and cemetery service, which helped me feel connected, but it was tough not being there in person with the family. I needed help with mucus in my trach and called for a respiratory therapist. Despite being busy, he cleared it and noticed I was emotional watching the service. He knelt by my bedside, held my hand, and watched the rest of the service with me, showing incredible kindness. I will always remember his compassion.

The following day, I successfully weaned for 17 and a half hours on the trach collar. The medical staff deemed me prepared to attempt breathing on my own through the night, which was scheduled for that evening. I was determined and fully prepared for the challenge. My bloodwork showed positive results, with my hemoglobin at 8.9, a good level for me. I was moved to a recliner to provide a change from being in the hospital bed. Physical therapy focused on strengthening my leg and foot muscles. Family members continued to visit me daily, offering encouragement and support as I persevered through my recovery journey.

Over the next two days, I remained on the trach collar continuously. I successfully completed 48 hours on the trach collar, with the ventilator being switched off during this time. I was now relying solely on oxygen assistance for breathing. Just one more day to reach the required 72-hour milestone. Following this, the medical team would consider permanently turning off the ventilator. Had I finally reached a stage in my journey that I never thought possible? Would there be unexpected challenges ahead that could delay my progress once again? I fervently prayed that this would be the breakthrough moment we had been anticipating. The next phase would involve capping the trach tube while keeping it in place.

The number 24 has always been a lucky number for Tom and me. It was the date of our wedding and now holds special significance for another reason. On October 24th, I reached the 72-hour mark on the trach collar. After seven and a half months, I no longer require the ventilator to breathe! The ventilator was disconnected, and taken out of my room. The feeling of not having to focus on breathing is indescribable. For the past seven and a half months, every breath was a conscious effort. Inhale through my nose, exhale through my mouth. Smell the flowers, blow out the candles. Breathing now feels effortless.

After the tube was capped, I had to adjust my breathing pattern to breathe in and out through my mouth. This was more challenging than it seemed. Prior to capping the tube, I was required to use a speaking valve for 72 hours. Despite attempts to use the valve intermittently, I could not tolerate it for more than 8 hours at a time. Breathing with the speaking valve felt different. On the day of capping, I could only manage to use the valve for 5 minutes, which was disappointing. I wondered if this setback would hinder my progress. Additionally, I had to learn to manage my airways without suctioning my secretions. Instead, I had to cough or spit them up on my own.

On October 26th, Sue had a challenging visit with me. When she arrived that night, I was coughing intensely and bringing up secretions from my lungs. The respiratory therapist helped clear some of it but then advised me to manage it on my own. Sue, my kind sister, sat by my side and assisted in removing the phlegm from my trach tube. I struggled to cough it out, so she helped by pulling it out with tissues. It may sound unpleasant, but my coughing was so intense that the secretions would fly across the room if my trach hole wasn't covered. Sue truly earned the title of the best sister that night!

It was decided my current tube was irritating my throat, and the decision was made to change the trach from a number 4 cuffed to a number 4 uncuffed tube. I gave all the praise to my outstanding respiratory therapist, Bill, as this was his idea to change the trach tube. He was so in tune with what I needed and had been the number one person at the hospital who I trusted. As soon as they changed the trach that morning, I had instant relief. I felt like I could breathe so much better and had less coughing. I tolerated 12 hours with the trach tube capped. They planned to keep it capped until bedtime. I asked the staff if they could keep it capped overnight, but they said no, that I was not ready for that yet. The plan was to cap the trach during the day, put the trach collar on overnight so I could get a good night's sleep and then cap the trach again in the morning. They kept stressing the importance of getting good sleep as my body needed it. Tom visited me, and I had a whole new perspective.

I expressed my gratitude to Tom numerous times for his encouragement and support in helping me stay positive and motivated to work hard. I felt a significant improvement in my condition. For the first time in nearly eight months, I was able to breathe through my mouth and nose like a normal person. The trach tube cap forced me to breathe naturally, which was a wonderful and liberating experience. Tom had been in contact with the inpatient rehab center, and they had already approved my admission to their rehabilitation program. They would admit me once I had successfully completed 48 hours with the trach tube capped and then removed. During physical therapy sessions, I was learning how to use a transfer board to move from my bed to a wheelchair. The staff wheeled me around the department, and it was a refreshing change to be out of my room. That evening, Courtney came to visit me, and we had a fantastic time together. I was in high spirits, and it was a joy to have such a positive day. I felt that moments like these were important for my children, family, and friends to witness as a reward for their prayers and concern for me.

On October 28, my trach tube was capped all day, as well as the day before and overnight. It remained capped, and if I could keep it that way overnight, I would meet my requirements. The medical team decided to keep the trach in for a few more days to ensure my respiratory stability. Although I still had my feeding tube, I was no longer receiving nutrition through it but was eating normally.

The following day, I was given Robitussin with codeine due to a cough and intermittent side pain. During therapy, I transitioned onto my wheelchair using a slide board and was able to propel the wheelchair myself by using my hands on the wheels navigating through the department and hallways, which gave me a sense of independence.

With my breathing improving, the focus shifted to my feet. Prolonged bed rest had caused a drop foot in both feet, resembling a ballerina's stance. Despite my efforts to move my toes, they remained immobile. The doctor noted limited movement when trying to position my feet at a 90-degree angle. Some toes showed discoloration due to poor circulation during ECMO. The medical team instructed the therapist to increase my mobility to enhance blood flow to my feet.

After eight months, I was finally able to wear clothes from home, marking a significant milestone in my recovery journey.

Over the last weekend in October, Tom traveled to Virginia with most of my family to celebrate my nephew Josh's wedding to our lovely new family member, Tasmia. I had hoped to be discharged from the hospital in time for the wedding, but unfortunately, that didn't happen. Throughout the weekend, my family kept me updated with photos and videos of the festivities. Tom enjoyed his weekend getaway without worrying about me, although he admitted that I was always on his mind.

While they were away, I had the opportunity to receive different visitors. Tom's sister, Angie, came up on Saturday for a visit. It was the first time I had seen her since I went into the hospital in March. She shared pictures of her beautiful grandchildren, and we discussed the recent passing of their mother a few weeks ago. It was wonderful to see her. On the day of the wedding, Luke and Natalie visited me together. My nephew, Bubba, live-streamed the wedding service, and Luke, Natalie, and I watched it together from the comfort of my hospital room. Natalie also trimmed the remaining strands of my hair, which were sparse and unkempt. I had never had a short haircut before, so it was a new experience for me.

On November 1st, a significant event occurred - my trach was removed! I had anticipated it would be painful, but the procedure turned out to be quite simple. I was left with a small hole in my neck that would heal on its own without the need for stitches, which was unexpected. The only remaining tube was a feeding tube, which was no longer in use. It had to be kept in place for a few more weeks despite not being used.

I had a wound specialist clean and scrub the tops of my feet to remove the scabby skin. This was quite painful. The entire top of my left foot had open wounds and scabs, making it very sensitive. Cleaning the sores on my feet was essential for the healing process. Honey was applied to cover the wounds and aid in healing after cleaning. The doctor prescribed antibiotics again because some areas on my feet were weeping and bleeding from the scraping, showing signs of infection.

I was diligently undergoing physical therapy to prepare for my upcoming physical rehabilitation. My discharge from the long-term rehab hospital was on November 5th. I successfully used a transfer board to move from my bed to the wheelchair independently. However, I could only sit upright with my feet dangling for a short time due to swelling and bleeding. The therapists also guided me to the gym, where I was assisted in standing at the parallel bars twice for about a minute each time.

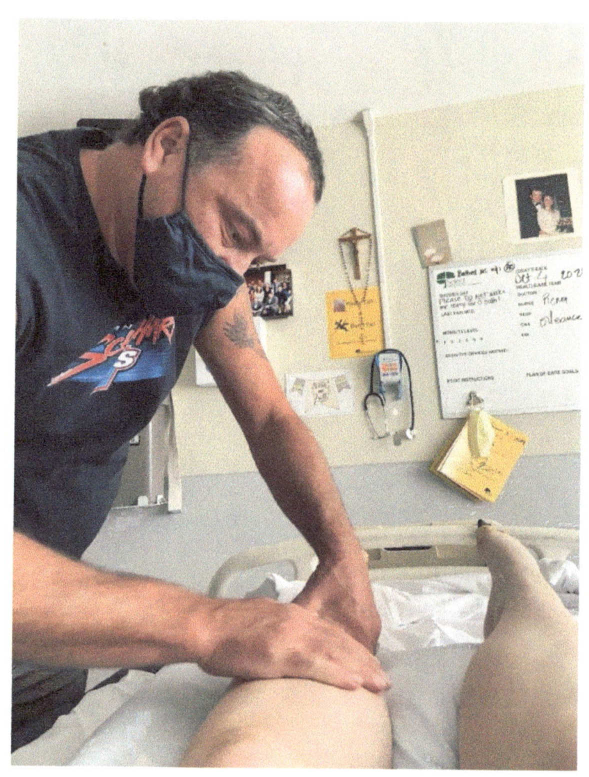

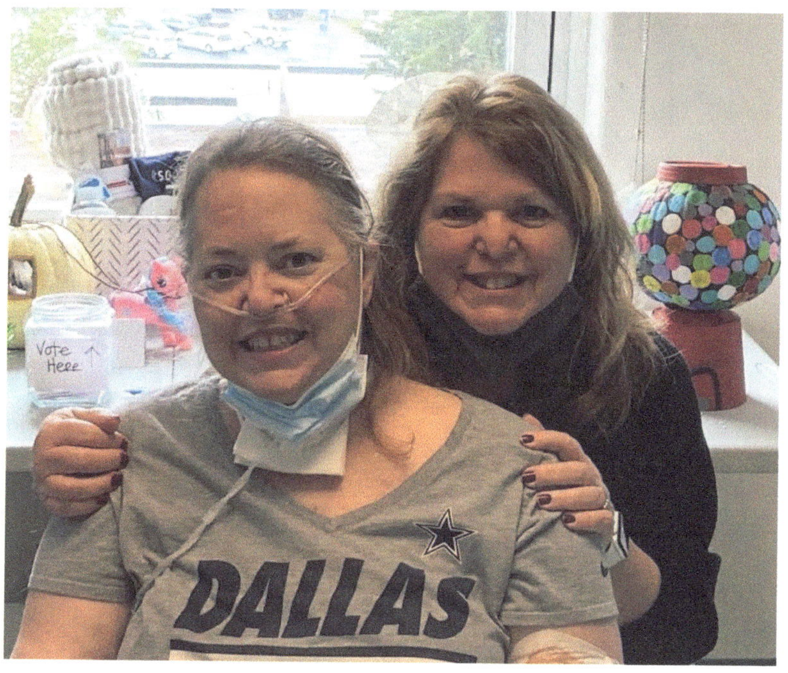
Vote Here
DALLAS

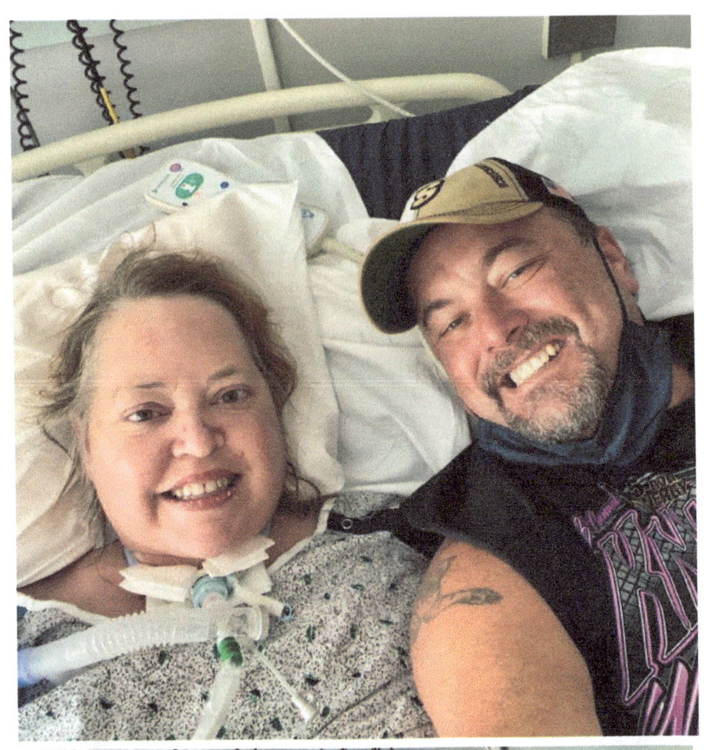

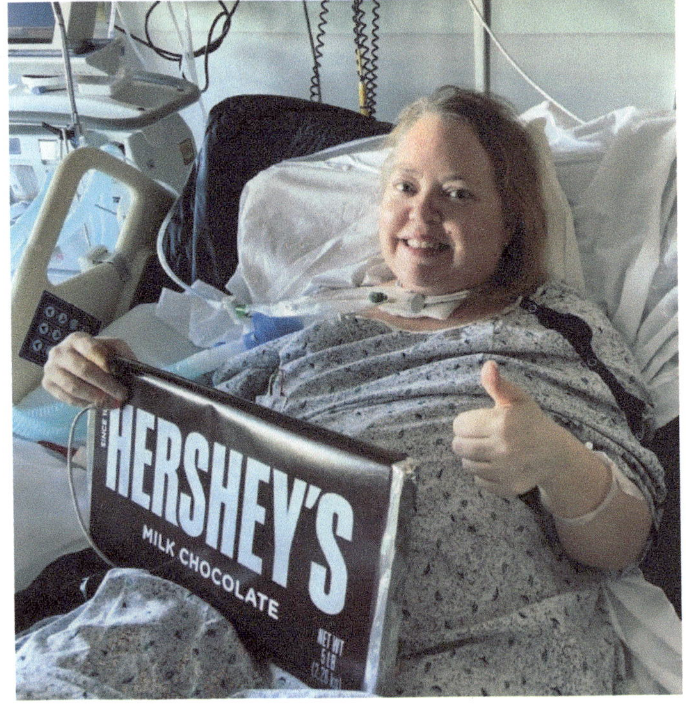
HERSHEY'S
MILK CHOCOLATE
NET WT

CHAPTER 12
REHABILITATION

In medical terms, rehabilitation is the process of restoring lost mental and/or physical abilities to enable normal or near-normal functioning. The rehabilitation hospital we chose had a fitting slogan on their website: "restoring hope, restoring lives." The main objectives of rehabilitation include restoring physical, emotional, and cognitive functions, managing pain, and enhancing quality of life. This all resonated well with me!

On November 6th, I was transferred from the long-term rehab hospital to the inpatient rehab. Before leaving the long-term facility, the doctor removed my feeding tube, making me tube-free as I entered rehab. They also treated the skin on my trach site, which had healed with some issues on the top, to help it develop better. Sue and Courtney packed my belongings and saw me off in the ambulance. I bid a tearful farewell to my favorite pulmonologist and my respiratory therapist, Bill, whose caring nature and positive outlooks had a profound impact on me. They not only improved me physically but also mentally. As a gesture of gratitude, I colored one last page from my "adult coloring book" for my physical therapist and left it under their door. I'm sure they had a good laugh when they found it the next day! The entire team at the long-term rehab was amazing and played a crucial role in my emotional recovery. They got to see more of my personality than any other hospital I had been to so far.

The ambulance ride to the inpatient rehab was comfortable as I didn't have a trach or need a ventilator. I had a pleasant conversation with the ambulance crew and admired the view outside the window during the journey. The visiting rules at the new rehab allowed only one visitor per day, and it had to be the same person. So, I was limited to seeing Tom for two hours each day.

The staff at the rehabilitation center were incredibly welcoming. Many of them had already familiarized themselves with my medical history and were genuinely excited to meet me. When my doctor entered the room, he immediately exclaimed, "I'm witnessing a miracle." He explained that very few individuals reached the stage of recovery that I had achieved. This sentiment was echoed by staff at every hospital I had been to, but it was only now sinking in for me. I realized that I was one of the fortunate few who had battled long-term COVID and emerged victorious. It made me believe that there must be a greater purpose for me to fulfill, as God had evidently kept me alive for a reason.

On the first day of my rehabilitation, I had appointments with occupational, physical, and speech therapists to assess my abilities. During lunch, I met with the speech therapist, who observed my eating, swallowing, and speech. I finished my meal and conversed with her throughout the session. After an hour, she determined that I did not require speech therapy. The physical and occupational therapists also visited me in my room, asked me questions to understand my situation, and assessed my abilities.

One great thing about the rehab hospital was that I didn't have to wear hospital gowns anymore! Tom brought clothes from home for me, and it confirmed what I always thought; he has no idea what I usually wear and doesn't look at what matches! Despite that, I appreciated his effort and happily sat in bed wearing my own clothes. The rehab facility helped me become more independent - I no longer needed nurses to bathe me. A nurse assisted me in getting into a wheelchair and taking me to the bathroom, where I brushed my teeth at the sink. Looking at myself in the mirror for the first time in a while, I brushed what was left of my hair and washed myself with a washcloth from a basin. This was a significant improvement from doing everything in my hospital bed. Tom's visiting hours were initially 6-8 pm, but due to his difficulty driving in the dark, we requested an exception from the hospital. They agreed, and he was allowed to visit from 3-5 pm every day, which made it easier for him.

The food at the rehab hospital was excellent. I relished the opportunity to order a diverse range of dishes now that I had the freedom to choose. I rediscovered the delicious flavors of coffee, ice cream, chocolate, and even salad. Despite losing around 65 pounds during my hospitalization, which was necessary, I felt it was okay to indulge in some treats and potentially gain a few pounds back.

On the second day of my rehabilitation, I began with occupational therapy. My therapist, Ally, was incredibly kind. She scheduled our session early in the day and assisted me with personal care tasks in my room, such as dressing, bathing, and grooming. Towards the end of the session, we also did some upper-body exercises. After a short break, I had a session with my physical therapist, Bobby. He wrapped my feet to protect them from dirt and infection, starting with a Vaseline wrap to prevent sticking, followed by multiple layers of gauze for cushioning and an oversized slipper sock to prevent falls. Bobby then helped me transfer to a wheelchair and took me to the gym, which had a bright and active atmosphere with a wall of windows that brought in natural light. It was the closest I had been to the outdoors in months, and the warmth of the sun on my skin was indescribable. In the gym, I did some light weight lifting and practiced standing using parallel bars. By shifting more weight onto my "good" right foot, I was able to stand for an impressive 1 minute and 45 seconds!

During the first week of rehabilitation, I underwent occupational therapy and physical therapy sessions twice a day. I had breaks in between to rest, which was much needed. Bobby took me outside after one session, and I enjoyed soaking up the sun on a warm November afternoon, which was rejuvenating. In the gym, there was a makeshift car where we practiced transferring in and out using a transfer board. Climbing inclines was challenging, requiring the correct technique and full strength to prevent sliding down. It felt like climbing a sliding board from childhood. These skills were essential for independent living at home. Bobby increased my stretching and weightlifting to strengthen my core and muscles. I also had the opportunity to interact with Norwood, the therapy dog, during a session. Playing fetch with Norwood for 30 minutes was not only enjoyable but also engaged various muscle groups. Bobby pointed out how activities like bending over to pick up the ball and throwing it were beneficial exercises that I wouldn't have been able to do a few weeks ago.

On Friday, November 11th, I received my first COVID-19 vaccine. I was a little anxious about getting it as I didn't want to fall ill and face a setback. However, after all I've been through, I knew it was necessary, and I welcomed it eagerly. Fortunately, I experienced no side effects from the shot, which was a huge relief.

During my therapy sessions, it became evident that the foot injuries I sustained would hinder my progress in walking as rapidly as initially anticipated. Consequently, the discharge plan was revised, and I was advised to return home with a wheelchair. Our therapy sessions focused on preparing me for this situation. However, this adjustment did not imply that we ceased efforts to improve my ability to stand and strengthen my legs or that I would not eventually regain the ability to walk. It simply meant that this milestone would take longer to achieve than originally expected.

On November 14th, I received the news I had been eagerly anticipating. My expected release date was set for November 24th, just in time for Thanksgiving! Our focus shifted to preparing the house for my return. We considered options like a chair lift or ramp to navigate the steps in our bilevel home. Tom assessed the doorways to ensure they were wide enough for a wheelchair. I had been using an inclined hospital bed for nine months to aid my breathing, so Tom bought an adjustable bed for me. The rehab facility assisted us in acquiring a wheelchair, shower chair, and potty chair.

Before I got home, my meticulous sisters had already cleaned the house from top to bottom. Tom had been trying to keep things in order, but the house was in need of a thorough cleaning. Tom and the rest of the family were also busy planning a memorable homecoming for me.

During the second week of therapy, Bobby focused on wheelchair agility with me. He would arrange orange cones for me to navigate around, improving my wheelchair-driving skills. I found myself more adept at maneuvering the wheelchair than my car! I also mastered using all the wheelchair features, such as applying the brakes and removing and reattaching the legs of the chair. Bobby and Ally set ambitious goals for my therapy, motivating me to work hard to achieve them and return home. One day, Bobby challenged me to independently complete the entire therapy session. I successfully transitioned from bed to wheelchair, wheeled myself to the gym, and began the workout routine, pushing myself to accomplish the task solo.

A few days before my release date, Tom was invited to join me in therapy. I was thrilled to showcase my progress, especially my improved wheelchair skills. Bobby and Ally demonstrated safe techniques to help me transition between surfaces and maneuver the wheelchair effectively. I introduced Tom to Norwood, the adorable therapy dog in the gym, as we both share a love for animals. After meeting Tom, Ally and Bobby were reassured about my care at home, seeing his dedication to my well-being.

On November 18th, I reached another significant milestone. The doctors gave me the green light to take a shower, and with Ally's help, I had my first one. In my bathroom, there was a handicapped shower seat, so she wheeled me over to it, and I used my transfer board to get on. The shower had a pull-down shower head that I used. I must have sat there for at least thirty minutes, just enjoying the warm water cascading over me. It was a wonderful feeling to finally have a proper shower and wash my hair. It's hard to put into words the sense of accomplishment that comes from something as simple as taking a shower after months without one. This routine task used to be so ordinary for me, but now it felt like a luxury or a reward for all the hard work I had put into my rehabilitation.

The nurses and doctors were working on reducing my oxygen intake from the 1 liter I was still on. Unfortunately, my oxygen saturation kept dropping when the level was lowered below 1 liter. We decided to arrange for oxygen delivery to the house in preparation for my return home.

One significant challenge remaining was transitioning from using a bedpan to using the bathroom. This step was highly anticipated for me personally. The idea of relying on a bedpan for so many months was still embarrassing to me. I found myself apologizing to the nurses almost every time I needed to use it. As a proud adult, the last thing you want is for someone else to take care of your waste. Ally placed a potty chair over the toilet and showed me how to use the transfer board to move onto the chair. I was thrilled when this milestone was achieved. Battling an illness teaches humility, and I was relieved to bid farewell to this aspect of my struggle.

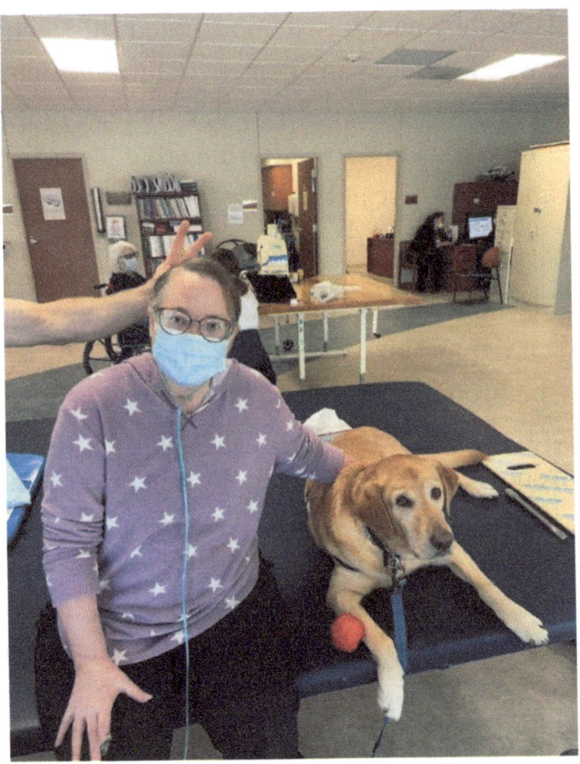

CHAPTER 13
I'M COMING HOME!

Wednesday, November 24th, 2021. Our lucky #24 struck again. A day I will never forget as long as I live; the day I finally went home. As soon as I woke up, I was super pumped up with excitement. There were no mixed emotions on this day! I couldn't wait to go home to be with my family!

I typed a Facebook message that morning:

The past 268 days have been the most challenging of my life but also filled with blessings and miracles. The rollercoaster of dealing with COVID-19 brought me through many highs and lows, but thanks to God's grace, I made it through. This experience has taught me valuable lessons about myself, my family, and the kindness of strangers. I am grateful for the amazing medical teams at five different hospitals who helped me recover. My faith has been strengthened, and I have witnessed the growth of faith in those closest to me. I am excited about what the future holds for us. A heartfelt thank you to all my supporters for their prayers, cards, messages, and visits. Your love and support have been my lifeline. Here's to the future!

My family had a grand homecoming celebration prepared, fit for royalty! My sisters came early in the morning to adorn the exterior of our house with balloons, homemade signs featuring pictures of loved ones, colorful streamers, and a welcoming home sign crafted by my nephew, Ryan.

Tom woke up that morning feeling like the light at the end of the tunnel was finally within reach. The day was as significant as our wedding day and the birth of our children. He described the excitement in my sisters' eyes upon their arrival as reminiscent of a child on Christmas morning, overwhelmed with joy. Grateful and reflecting on the challenging journey that led to this moment, he felt a profound sense of unconditional love that was truly incredible. The uncertainty of a second chance at life with the one you love makes every moment even more precious.

The nurse came into my room in the morning and assisted me with my personal care tasks. I took the extra step of putting in my contacts and applying a bit of makeup, which I hadn't done in 9 months. I ordered a new sweatshirt online from my favorite boutique, Lady Lily Boutique, and put it on. The nurse helped me pack all my personal items, which was the 6th time they had been packed, but this time, they were being delivered to my house, not another hospital room. The nurse brought in my list of medications and went over it with me. When I was admitted to the hospital in March, I was only on two blood pressure medications. Now, I was leaving with a total of 17 medications and supplements. The therapist came in and wrapped my feet carefully to protect them during the trip home. They used Vaseline wraps as a base, followed by thick gauze around my feet and ankles, and then slipper socks on top. Due to the swelling and sensitivity of my feet from the sores left by ECMO, I couldn't wear shoes or slippers yet. I couldn't put much weight on my feet and had to be careful not to let them hang down for too long to avoid bleeding and pain. My new wheelchair and potty chair were delivered to the hospital, and they were packed with my belongings.

As I lay on the bed in my hospital room, I looked around at the packed-up space and felt grateful to have reached this point in my journey. I couldn't help but think that God must have some significant plans for me if he had kept me alive through such a challenging experience. What would life look like for me once I returned home? Tom had been living alone for nine months, and we joked that he would have to give up his bachelor ways when I came back. No more drinking out of the milk container or leaving the toilet seat up! He jokingly claimed he never got the memo that he couldn't act like a bachelor. I knew that taking care of me would require effort, and I hoped it wouldn't overwhelm Tom.

My thoughts also turned to my mom, Kathleen, and my mother-in-law, Ellen. Going back to a life without either of them felt empty. I imagined seeing them both when I arrived home, but the reality was that they were no longer there. The mourning for their loss had not fully set in yet.

Back at our house, my sisters were just finishing up decorating while my nephew, Bubba, arrived to video the day's events. They were excited to see the limousine pulling up outside. My sisters were thrilled, clapping and smiling as they saw the limo arrive. Lori mentioned it was her first time in a limo. The limo could accommodate eight people, so we had planned for Bubba, Tom, myself, and my three sisters, leaving two seats and foot space for other items. My sisters packed the limo with coolers of juice and champagne for mimosas, food for charcuterie boards, beer for Tom, balloons, and signs they made for me. They never travel lightly and always have all the details covered! They loaded into the limo and headed off on the hour-long ride to the rehab center to pick me up. Along the way, they reminisced about the past year and what this homecoming meant to them. They FaceTimed me so I could share in the excitement. Bubba was enjoying the limo experience, capturing the fun moments and coordinating with news stations covering my homecoming. As we approached the hospital, Tom expressed his anticipation of bringing his love home. The excitement of what was to come next was palpable.

In my room, hospital staff came to update me on the day's plans. They mentioned that a news station would be covering the "clap out" they had organized. A clapout involves hospital staff cheering as I leave the building. I signed some consent forms and discussed potential press questions. The prospect of going home was starting to feel real.

Tom, Bubba, and my sisters stepped out of the limo and headed into the hospital. After checking in, only Tom was allowed to accompany me to my room. My sisters remained at the hospital entrance, where they joined a growing group of staff. As Tom made his way down the hallway towards my room, he was filled with excitement and anticipation. The moment felt surreal, and he couldn't help but feel a sense of wonder. Walking through the hospital corridors, he realized that after nine months of navigating them alone, this time, he would be leaving with me, taking me home. It was a moment he had dreamed of. Once we received the green light from the hospital staff, I transferred to my wheelchair, connected to the portable oxygen tank, and Tom, along with the nurses, gathered my belongings. As we made our way towards the exit, we turned a corner and saw a line of doctors and heard the noise of what seemed like a lively crowd. The nurses pushing the wheelchair chuckled, remarking that they hadn't expected to be on TV that day and would have dressed up a bit more if they had known.

When I arrived at the hospital entrance, the first people I noticed were my doctor and his assistant. As I turned the corner, I was greeted by a crowd of 25-30 people, including a camera crew and a reporter, all clapping and cheering. My nurse gently guided me through the lineup as I waved at familiar faces and soaked in the moment. At the end of the line, I spotted my two favorite therapists, Allie and Bobbie, as well as my three sisters. I was overwhelmed with excitement, reminding myself to breathe. I embraced each of my sisters, then my therapists, before joining Tom for an interview with the news crew. After the interview, I was wheeled outside, where I spotted a dear friend and her parents in the crowd. They had come to see me off, a touching gesture as they lived closer to the hospital than my home.

After stepping outside, we were greeted by the sight of the long limousine parked right in front of us. It was quite a luxurious way to head home! We had to make sure the wheelchair and potty chair fit in the back of the limo. A few balloons had to be popped to make room for all of us, along with the coolers and posters. With the transfer board in hand, we carefully maneuvered me from the wheelchair into the limo. Once settled inside, the party kicked off! Champagne bottles were popped, and plates of food kept coming around. We enjoyed music, drinks, food, and endless conversations. It had been nine months since the four sisters had a chance to catch up, and it was a truly wonderful reunion! Bubba captured the moments on video, joining in the celebration while also keeping the news outlets updated as they gathered at our house. Meanwhile, Courtney, Luke, and their families were at home welcoming the groups of news crews, family, and friends who were eagerly awaiting my arrival. The atmosphere was filled with excitement and positivity!

Before we realized it, we were turning the corner into our neighborhood. Our neighbors were outside, ready to greet us as we passed by. We decided to take a detour through the development to visit Tom's stepmother and father's house to say hello. After exchanging hugs, we continued our drive and turned another corner, only to find cars parked everywhere. A large video sign on a truck caught our attention, flashing various greetings to welcome us home. The messages featured backgrounds like a casino and the Dallas Cowboys, all aimed at welcoming me back home.

As we turned the corner to enter our road, we were greeted by a crowd of people lining the street with signs, blowing horns, clapping, crying, and shouting, "Welcome home." My sister-in-law, Gina, had her van decorated with welcoming messages. Cousins, aunts, uncles, nieces, nephews, friends, coworkers, neighbors, my family, and most importantly, my grandkids were all there with homemade signs, eagerly waiting to welcome me home. The overwhelming emotion I experienced was indescribable. The air was filled with love and support. The limo driver beeped the horn as we approached our house. My 7-year-old grandson, Knox, turned to his mother and said, "Mommy, I'm shaking," capturing the excitement of the moment. When the limo came to a stop, I opened the door and motioned for my grandkids to come over for a hug. Knox and Lincoln ran over, and I embraced them tightly, savoring the moment and feeling grateful to have them in my arms again. They had grown so much, and it was a joy to hold them close once more.

The children stepped back from the limo as four news station cameras were positioned around the car door. The first reporter began asking me questions about my recovery journey. I shared that I had never thought I would make it back home, but I never lost hope. The road to recovery had its share of highs and lows, earning it the nickname 'COVID coaster'. I emphasized the importance of my support system, prayer warriors, and family in helping me through. My faith had strengthened, and I expressed eternal gratitude to God for granting me a second chance at life. I advised others on a similar journey to be patient, have faith, follow medical advice, be open to new treatments, and work on managing anxieties. I acknowledged my husband as my rock and stressed the importance of taking things one step at a time. I praised the medical staff for their invaluable support, both medically and emotionally, during challenging times.

During my interview, the rest of the group exited the limo and began unpacking, preparing my wheelchair, and warmly welcoming the crowd of friends and family. It was a joyous celebration for all. After the interviews concluded, Tom assisted me in using the transfer board to move from the seat to my wheelchair. It had been a while since I had been outdoors, so he covered me up to keep me warm. He then pushed me to the sidewalk, where I was surrounded by a sea of familiar faces who had supported me through my illness. Initially, we had planned not to have physical contact with anyone due to COVID-19 concerns, but my heart had other ideas. I gestured for a hug to the first friend I saw, and she embraced me without hesitation. This sparked a chain reaction, and I greeted as many people in the crowd as I could reach. The atmosphere was filled with picture-taking, video recording, hugs, and tears. A drone even captured aerial footage of the event, adding to the excitement. The effort put into the handmade signs held by everyone was truly remarkable. News crews stayed to interview numerous family members, making it a day that will be etched in everyone's memory forever!

After navigating through the crowd, I bid farewell and entered the house with my immediate family through the garage. The reality of my physical limitations quickly set in. How would we manage to get the wheelchair over the doorstep? How could I transition from the wheelchair to the chair lift? These were challenges we hadn't practiced for. After some trial and error, we positioned the transfer board correctly to assist me onto the chair lift. My son and nephew then struggled to fold the wheelchair and transport it to the front of the house, up two flights of stairs, to make it accessible upstairs. I ascended the first flight of steps using the chair lift. We then had to figure out the transition between the two lifts, as my house is bi-level. Tom fetched a wheeled chair from the garage, and we nervously transferred from one lift chair to the wheelchair to the other lift chair. I then took the second chair lift to the top floor and transferred back to my wheelchair. A final transfer to the couch allowed me to relax at home finally. Tom, our children, and grandchildren enjoyed each other's company once again. My siblings, nieces, and nephews gradually arrived, ensuring that all our needs were met. A news crew entered our home and provided a live update from our living room, adding to the excitement. We gathered around, switching between different news stations to watch the coverage of the homecoming. That night, Facebook was flooded with everyone's photos, videos, and well-wishes for us. It was a truly unforgettable and heartwarming day.

Welcome Home
Mom
We Love You!
WELCOME
HOME
JUL
Downtown
Julie Brown
Takes Rona
Down!

CHAPTER 14
OUR NEW AND IMPROVED LIFE

After the news crews and family had left, it was just Tom and me in the house. We were both exhausted but couldn't stop smiling and talking about the day's events. We eagerly looked forward to crawling into bed together, but things were not as simple as they used to be. Every task required planning and preparation now that I was in a wheelchair. We had to carefully navigate the process of transferring me from the wheelchair to the bed, which took a lot of effort and coordination. It was a new experience for me, as I was used to having rails on my bed to assist with movement. Tom never complained, but I could tell he had a lot on his plate with me being home.

The rehabilitation hospital organized a nurse, occupational therapist, and physical therapist to visit our home and provide assistance. The first to arrive was our nurse, who we discovered was a distant family member, which was reassuring. During each visit, she checked my vital signs and addressed any medical concerns we had. After a week, she took a blood sample to ensure my levels were within the appropriate range, which they were. As I was progressing well, we only required her services for a few weeks.

We were assigned an occupational therapist named Barb, who provided valuable assistance in navigating the house with a wheelchair and carrying out daily tasks. She offered suggestions on the type of shower chair I required and provided guidance on using the potty chair more effectively. To facilitate wheelchair access, Tom removed the bathroom door, making it easier to maneuver in and out, although turning the wheelchair around tight corners without damaging the walls or getting stuck remained a challenge. For the next few months, the bathroom only offered privacy through a curtain, as the door had been removed.

During our rotation, we had the opportunity to work with several physical therapists, but one in particular stood out to us. Deena, an engaging and motivating therapist, quickly became our favorite, and we requested to work with her exclusively. She would massage my legs and feet and guide me through exercises to activate the muscles necessary for the next phase of my rehabilitation.

Receiving daily visits from family and friends was a great comfort. Tom and I began to share our experiences with others, sparking interesting conversations as people recalled things I had mentioned in the hospital, triggering memories of events and dreams. Sue had printed all the emails she had sent during my hospital stay, and as I read them, I noticed that they didn't always reflect the seriousness of my situation. Sue and Tom explained that this was intentional - they wanted to maintain a positive and upbeat tone in the emails to spare others from the emotional rollercoaster my family was experiencing.

Karen spearheaded a food committee that ensured we were well-nourished during my recovery. It was a delightful experience, allowing us to reconnect with friends and family over their delicious meals. Tom and I felt truly blessed each day as we eagerly anticipated who would be visiting our home to deliver dinner. We cherished the time spent with our guests, expressing our gratitude for their kindness. The acts of selflessness displayed by others were truly heartwarming. These initial weeks of assistance served as a powerful reminder of the faith and goodness present in the world, even for those who may have doubted it.

During the first few weeks, we had a lot of support from various helpers who assisted us with different aspects of daily life. Our house was cleaned, groceries were ordered online and picked up, laundry was taken care of, and snow was shoveled from our driveway. We didn't initially ask for this help, as we are proud individuals, but we recognized that we needed assistance during that challenging period, and it was readily available to us.

My first outing after staying indoors for a long time was to get my COVID-19 booster shot at the doctor's office. The journey there and back was tiring yet invigorating. Everyday sights that I had grown accustomed to over the past 50 years suddenly seemed more exciting. I observed every little change that had occurred in the past year.

Two weeks after returning home, I visited my workplace for a children's Christmas event with Luke and my two grandsons. It was a comforting experience to be back in the familiar environment where I had worked for 22 years, surrounded by colleagues I saw every day. My grandkids had a wonderful time, and Luke must have been relieved that he managed to get me there and back without any issues. I could sense the pressure on people tasked with assisting me, ensuring they knew how to handle the wheelchair oxygen tank and navigate wheelchair-accessible paths. Luke handled everything admirably. Later that day, Courtney and Megan joined us for our annual Christmas cookie-making tradition, although we missed having my mom, Kathleen, with us. Despite her absence, we had a great time and felt her presence as we cherished our time together. The following week, my sisters came over, and we made my mom's favorite Christmas candy together - chocolate-covered peanut butter crackers. With the help of assistants, we wrapped all the Christmas presents I had ordered online, and my longtime hairdresser friend Joanie made a house call to cut and color my new short hair.

Tom's long-awaited neck surgery was rescheduled from December 16th to January due to issues with his oxygen saturation. Further testing was required to ensure his well-being, but the results came back normal. The doctor attributed the inaccurate readings to years of finger pricks as a diabetic. Despite the delay, we believed it happened for a reason, as I still depended on Tom for daily tasks. Tom also felt that both families had endured a challenging year and deserved a peaceful Christmas season.

Energy conservation has become a crucial aspect of my daily routine. With limited energy resources, it is essential to prioritize tasks effectively. After my daily rehab visits, I often needed an afternoon nap to recharge. The wheelchair transfers required for bathroom visits demanded significant energy, making it a top priority. Getting into bed at night was also a challenging task. If I didn't conserve enough energy, Tom had to assist me, which was exhausting for him. I realized the importance of managing these tasks independently before his surgery.

We made the most of our Christmas, feeling incredibly thankful for the gift of life. While we cherished the presence of our supportive family members, we deeply felt the absence of our moms, who always made holidays special. My kids prepared a wonderful Christmas breakfast to celebrate Tom's birthday, which falls on Christmas Day. The grandkids added to the joy of the day with their infectious excitement while unwrapping presents.

A month after returning home, I progressed in my rehabilitation to the point where I could start standing. To reach this milestone, I focused on strengthening the muscles in my arms and legs and improving the sensitivity in my feet to be able to wear socks or shoes. My physical therapist, Deena, helped desensitize my feet by using various objects like a cold-water bottle, silk fabric, and a hairbrush to gradually build up tolerance for wearing socks. It took trying out 4-5 different socks and orthopedic shoes before finding a slip-on clog that provided the support I needed to stand. On December 29th, I stood for the first time at home, marking a significant achievement for me. Determined to start the new year on both feet, on New Year's Eve at 11:59 p.m., with the help of Tom and Kenny, I stood up while on FaceTime with my family as they witnessed me welcoming 2022 standing tall.

January was a month filled with significant changes for me. During the first week, I made progress in standing and taking steps with my walker. Deena, my physical therapist, focused on massaging my foot muscles and treating the sore on my toes, which showed improvement. Barb, my occupational therapist, helped me with tasks like showering independently, dressing myself, and managing personal grooming. This allowed Tom to be relieved from the task he disliked the most - choosing my clothes.

Tom had his neck fusion surgery on January 12th. Our kids helped take him to the hospital and stayed with me overnight. The surgery was successful, although he had some blood pressure issues initially. After resolving that, he was discharged the day after the surgery. He came home with a neck brace that he had to wear for 4-5 weeks and a weight restriction of 5 pounds. It was challenging having two people unable to do much, but we had a lot of support from prayer warriors and supporters who helped us through this tough time.

I had a second interview with a local news station where we discussed the challenges of being in the hospital for nine months, the treatments I underwent, and my outlook for the future. Despite the loneliness, I remained positive and confident about a full recovery. I also emphasized the importance of vaccination in reducing the impact of the disease. If you haven't already, consider getting vaccinated.

By the end of January, I was using a walker to move around inside the house. While I still relied on a wheelchair for longer distances outdoors, I could feel the progress from the in-home therapy sessions. On January 30th, my sisters and I had our first outing together at Sue's house. We enjoyed a lovely lunch and spent the afternoon going through some items they had saved from our parents' house. We had meaningful conversations about our experiences from the past year, making it a therapeutic afternoon for all of us.

I also began working on a book detailing my hospitalization experience. Sue had made a good start by compiling emails, and I added my perspective, emotions, and additional details that were not included in the emails. I meticulously reviewed every hospital note from each facility and sifted through emails, texts, Facebook posts, cards, and hospital e-cards received over the past year. I interviewed numerous individuals to gather their accounts of my time in the hospital. It was fascinating to uncover a part of my life that I had largely slept through, as experienced by my family and friends.

My feet remained my greatest physical challenge. I had developed neuropathy in them, causing constant pain. My doctors explained that this was a common side effect for patients who spent extended periods in a hospital bed, and unfortunately, there were limited treatment options available.

It took Tom approximately three weeks to navigate the most challenging phase of his recovery from neck surgery. He experienced significant pain, and the neck brace he had to wear was extremely uncomfortable. Adhering to the restriction of not lifting more than 5 pounds was particularly difficult for him. It was unnatural for Tom to witness my struggles and not be able to assist, but it was essential for his own healing process. In a way, his inability to help may have actually aided in my recovery, as I had to become more self-reliant and put an end to the pampering he had been providing since my return home.

After receiving numerous bills for hospital stays, ambulance transfers, medical devices, physical therapy, and Tom's surgery, my family and friends were given the green flag to organize a fundraiser to help alleviate the financial strain. The event is scheduled for March at a nearby club, and my loved ones are working diligently to ensure its success.

In February, my therapists began helping me walk up and down the steps of my house. It was a challenge as I discovered muscles I hadn't used in a while. They also had me start doing laundry, which was more exhausting than before. After therapy, I needed a nap to recover. I focused on sit-to-stand exercises to regain strength, even though it was difficult at first. By mid-month, I started using two canes instead of a walker, which took some time to adjust to due to my lack of coordination.

Since I hadn't seen a doctor in a while, I sought out specialists to address my long-term issues. The first doctor I visited was a pulmonologist. Sue kindly drove me to the appointment as neither Tom nor I could drive yet. The doctor was amazed by my recovery and conducted tests to assess my progress. A 6-minute walk test was completed to assess my need for continued oxygen. After 3 minutes, my saturation went below 90, so I remained on oxygen. A sleep study revealed the need for a sleep apnea machine. Sue and I stopped for ice cream on the way home, a treat I missed out on the year before.

My next appointment was with a highly recommended foot surgeon. Since Tom was still unable to drive, my brother Andy and his wife Belinda kindly took us to the appointment in York. The doctor ordered an x-ray and confirmed that the bones in my feet were in good condition. He reviewed the reports from Deena regarding the physical therapy we had been doing to address my drop foot. The doctor indicated that as long as I continued to progress with therapy, surgery on my feet should not be necessary. However, if my progress plateaued, we would need to revisit the option of surgery to cut my Achilles tendon to lengthen it and help with the drop foot. He prescribed Lyrica to assist with my neuropathy. His advice aligned with what I had been hearing from other doctors: "Let's wait and see how you progress." While it was reassuring that immediate treatment was not required, it was also frustrating that there were no immediate solutions to my medical issues. There was no clear guidance on how to manage long-term COVID-19 patients.

As March approached, we realized that it had been a year since I was hospitalized for COVID-19. Reflecting on the past year, it was filled with unexpected challenges and incredible support from God, family, friends, hospital staff, and even strangers. If someone had told me a year ago about everything I would go through and the unwavering support I would receive, I wouldn't have believed it. I never would have imagined that my once hot-headed and impatient husband would become a source of positivity, patience, and faith during the darkest times. Life has a way of surprising us, and that's what makes it so unpredictable and exciting. In the darkest moments, hope and positivity were my guiding lights.

To help me stay focused on my therapy goals, my occupational therapist, Barb, suggested setting a timer on my phone to remind me to move every hour. She encouraged me to increase my activity throughout the day, which included walking with two canes, preparing my own meals, and doing the prescribed exercises. Despite the persistent numbness in my shins and feet, I knew that following her advice was crucial for my recovery. So, every hour, the sound of 'You Shook Me All Night Long' by AC/DC would fill the house from the alarm on my phone. It was ironic that my favorite song had become a reminder for me to keep moving. Surprisingly, it was effective, and I noticed improvements in my condition as I became more active.

My next specialist appointment was with an orthodontist who specialized in making braces to help with foot drop. My in-home physical therapist, Deena, accompanied me and Tom to the visit. The orthodontist had me try on a stock pair of braces, and Deena lent me her larger sneakers to test walking - it was like a miracle! I was able to walk with significantly less pain and without the heavy, awkward gait I had before. I ordered a pair of braces that day and felt hopeful for a more 'normal' walking experience.

I hadn't been out in public much yet, so I was looking forward to some entertainment in my day. The first weekend in March, my dad's side of the family had a family reunion. With the help of a few family members, I enjoyed the day playing my favorite card game, Texas hold 'em, socializing, and expressing my gratitude to my family members who had prayed so hard for me during my illness. Karaoke was a tradition at our reunion, but I had to sit it out as I didn't have enough air in my lungs, and my throat was still scratchy and sore. That day marked a step back into life for me!

By mid-March, I had completed my in-home therapy with Barb and Deena. Tearful goodbyes were exchanged with these wonderful ladies who had supported me emotionally and physically throughout my journey. They both hold a special place in my heart, and I am incredibly grateful for their dedication to helping me become stronger.

On March 15th, I embarked on my first major trip of the year. Tom, myself, and five other couples traveled three hours to our annual vacation spot for St. Patrick's Day - Ocean City, MD. This time last year, I was in the hospital looking at old vacation photos, wishing for another chance to visit with friends. That wish came true. It was a fantastic weekend of bonding and relaxation with friends. We ate, drank, laughed, and reminisced like only lifelong friends can. It was truly rejuvenating for all of us!

The following week was focused on preparing for the next phase of my rehabilitation, which involved outpatient physical therapy and pulmonary therapy. I was juggling both therapies simultaneously. Additionally, I visited a podiatrist to address issues with my feet, particularly the skin on top and my COVID-19 toes. The podiatrist addressed ingrown toenails and properly treated the dead nails that hadn't fallen out. He also examined a toe with necrotic skin and advised me to wait and monitor the situation as the black caps provided better protection against infection. I collected my braces from the orthodontist and obtained a specially-sized shoe to accommodate them. The shoe was three sizes larger and triple wide to fit the brace, causing my foot to move around uncomfortably. Despite being advised to adjust the brace, I found the process frustrating and ultimately chose not to wear the braces. Instead, I focused on intensive therapy to address my drop foot without relying on the brace.

On March 19th, they held our fundraiser, and the organization of the event was flawless. My family, friends, and community showed incredible support, creating a day that will forever be etched in our memories. The day began with rows of raffle baskets filled with donations from various sources. A baked goods stand offered homemade treats made by loved ones for sale. The St. Patrick's Day theme was evident, with everyone dressed in green and green decorations adorning the hall. Tables displayed pictures of me and my family members, adding a personal touch to the event. The club sold gambling jar tickets, and there was a variety of donated food and drinks available for purchase throughout the day. My cousin and her husband generously provided pit beef, which they smoked outside the hall. Family members volunteered to manage the kitchen, raffles, and baked goods table. A Texas hold 'em tournament, organized by my cousin and her husband, added to the excitement. The club hosted a triathlon of cornhole, darts, and shuffle bowling upstairs, which was a popular activity. The hall was bustling with hundreds of people coming and going, creating a positive and loving atmosphere that was infectious. As the night came to a close, Tom and I addressed the crowd, expressing our gratitude for the overwhelming support and prayers we had received. The generosity and willingness to help those in need were truly humbling. The love and unity in the room that night left a lasting impact on everyone present. We are committed to paying forward the kindness we have received for the rest of our lives.

In late March, we were given a special opportunity by Select Specialty Hospitals to speak at a national conference for CEOs in San Diego, CA. They generously covered all our travel expenses, arranging for a town car to pick us up from our home and drive us to the airport. Upon arrival, a wheelchair was provided to assist us through security and to our gate for boarding. Flying first class, we were among the first to board and were seated in the front of the plane. The flight attendants offered us warm towels and drinks before the other passengers had even boarded. Throughout the 6-hour nonstop flight, we were served a delicious meal, warm nuts, dessert, and unlimited drinks. It was a delightful experience being pampered in this way. Upon landing in San Diego, a driver was waiting to take us to our hotel, conveniently located just across the street from the airport. After settling into our room, we decided to rest as my feet were swollen, and we were both exhausted. Our room had two balconies with stunning views of the water, allowing us to enjoy the sunrise, sunset, and the sight of beautiful boats right outside our hotel.

During our third day at the event, we had the opportunity to share our story with the audience. They were eager to hear about our journey and gave us complete freedom to speak without any restrictions. Although they offered to display our words on a teleprompter, we chose to speak from the heart without a prepared speech. We narrated our experiences from start to finish, captivating the audience of CEOs and doctors. You would have thought we would be nervous, but Tom and I comfortably talked for almost an hour and received multiple standing ovations!

We shared instances where we formed strong bonds with staff members, highlighted the exceptional efforts of overworked nurses and therapists who went above and beyond to care for me, and praised doctors for their compassionate bedside manner that positively impacted my recovery. We also candidly discussed some challenges we faced during the process, offering suggestions for improvement, especially in the transition to home care.

After being discharged from the hospital, I received in-home nursing visits once a week and therapy sessions 3-4 times a week. A week later, I had a video consultation with my primary doctor, who reviewed my medications and advised me to continue my current regimen. However, I felt that more follow-up appointments would have been beneficial to ensure a smoother transition to home care. I heavily relied on my care team, who were not medical professionals, for guidance, and they provided excellent support.

I proposed to the group that developing a more comprehensive discharge plan for patients transitioning to home care could be advantageous, and they were receptive to the suggestion. That evening, we enjoyed a dinner cruise with the group, savoring cocktails and delicious food while cruising around the stunning San Diego skyline. We had the pleasure of sitting with the CEOs of two hospitals where I had been hospitalized during COVID-19. Throughout the night, there was a line of people eager to engage in conversation with us. Doctor after doctor expressed that I was part of the 1% who had survived, a true miracle. Their eyes revealed the hardships they had faced and the exhaustion they felt. It was a humbling experience to be in the company of such resilient individuals, and it was a night we will always cherish.

On our final day in San Diego, we took an Uber to La Jolla Beach, a breathtaking area. We marveled at the sea lions lounging on the sand and rocks and the unique cliffs and rocky shoreline that differed from the east coast scenery we were accustomed to. We spent hours soaking up the sun and admiring the beauty of the surroundings. Overall, the vacation was a memorable experience, and we were grateful for the opportunity to be a part of it. The following day, we returned to the airport, feeling thankful for the chance to share our story.

Upon our return home, we took a few days to rest and ease back into our routine. I continued with outpatient therapy at both a pulmonary rehab and a physical therapy rehab. Fortunately, I had the privilege of working with two more exceptional groups of caregivers from April to September.

Pulmonary therapy worked on my stamina and upper body strength. The girls I met there were so supportive and made it exciting to come twice a week. A full circle moment happened when one of the respiratory therapists from my first hospital who saw me as I was declining, Amy, was now my respiratory therapist to build me back up. God works in mysterious ways! Unfortunately, I was not able to transition off the use of daily oxygen, but we sure tried! A visit back to my pulmonologist, along with a CAT scan, confirmed my lungs were still severely damaged.

The physical therapist worked to strengthen the larger muscle groups in my legs. They targeted my drop foot issue and had me transitioning from a walker to 2 canes to 1 cane to walking freely by the final day of therapy. My gratitude for this group of people who helped me work into a life I envisioned is tremendous. For once being told I would never walk again versus walking with no assistance is a dream come true. No one knows what the future holds for someone recovering from a long-term illness.

In August, we had a rare opportunity to attend an ECMO survivor dinner hosted by a regional hospital. The event took place at a beautiful location an hour away from our home. Upon arrival, we were warmly welcomed by one of the ECMO technicians, who was thrilled to see Tom again and to meet me for the first time. We also had the chance to meet the technician who performed CPR on me during a critical moment. It was surreal to hear their perspective on the events. I hope they found it rewarding to witness the positive outcome of their efforts.

As we mingled at the event, we headed to the bar for a drink, where I noticed a group of four men who seemed familiar. Upon closer inspection, I recognized the first man as the doctor who had conducted most of my bronchoscopies. I expressed my gratitude for his care. The next man I recognized was the thoracic surgeon who had operated on my right lung to remove the gel. I couldn't resist giving him a hug as a gesture of thanks for saving my life.

The doctors shared memories of my hospital stay, revealing that they had nicknamed me "Downtown" after a popular VJ from the 80s. It was a nickname they used when referring to me in discussions. I then met the head of the ECMO unit, who recalled seeing me when my heart had stopped and expressed his joy at seeing me thriving now. Another doctor from the ECMO team recounted a unique experience involving a risky procedure that ultimately saved my life. This Russian doctor had suggested an unconventional approach to address a clot near my collarbone, which resulted in a distinctive sunburst scar that serves as a reminder of their innovative intervention.

I am grateful to the medical team for their dedication, creativity, and unwavering commitment to my recovery. While I may not have the courage to get a traditional tattoo, I proudly bear the mark of their lifesaving efforts.

We then met some of the other ECMO technicians, who greeted me warmly. Tom was familiar with all of them, and they all praised Tom for his positive attitude and pleasant demeanor during my hospital stay. We engaged in conversations with several survivors who attended the event. Some had been on ECMO for only a week or two, while others, like me, had been on it for a longer period. The severe side effects of ECMO, such as poor circulation to the extremities, were more pronounced in some individuals than in others. It was a stark reminder of how fortunate I was to have a few long-term effects from my journey. Many survivors had experienced amputations of fingers, toes, or even parts of their feet and legs. Despite their challenges, they were all grateful for their current situation. I underwent the amputation of half of my right index finger and lost half of my middle toe on my right foot, but thankfully, these losses did not affect my functionality, for which I was immensely grateful.

During dinner, I conversed with four other survivors and the support team members accompanying them. Only in a group like ours could we openly discuss our shared experiences. Each of us had unique stories from the various facilities we had been treated at. While some memories were hazy, others vividly recalled the challenges of weaning off ventilators. We were a diverse group of individuals who had all survived an epidemic and emerged stronger. None of us had anticipated the profound impact a pandemic virus would have on our lives.

A presentation featured myself and two others, though every person present had a story worthy of being shared. We bid farewell to our newfound friends and the doctors who had played a crucial role in saving our lives. It was another remarkable evening where I had the privilege of expressing my gratitude to the exceptional medical professionals who had cared for me. I will forever be indebted to these skilled doctors and their dedicated support staff.

CHAPTER 15
THE 1%

The title "1%" came from a doctor at my rehab hospital who referred to me as a 1%er, meaning I had survived the worst of COVID-19. Another doctor in San Diego also mentioned the 1% who make it through the ECMO and ventilator phases of recovery. In COVID statistics, the 1% represents those who have overcome the virus. Meeting other survivors has shown me the strength and resilience of these individuals. The ECMO survivor dinner and support group have introduced me to some of the most inspiring and grateful people I have ever met. They focus on the future and appreciate each day they are given.

In comparison, below are some examples of 1% facts. You may be part of a 1% group!!

- 1% of NCAA basketball players make the NBA.
- 1% of the world's population has run a marathon.
- 1% of the world's population is vegetarian.
- 1% of the world's population has a twin sibling.
- 1% of the world's population is allergic to peanuts.
- 1% of the world's population has natural red hair.
- 1% of the world's population has AB Negative blood type.
- 1% of the people are born with green eyes.
- 1% of the wealthy people in the US in 2023 had a net worth of 13.7 million or more
- The earth is about 1% the diameter of the sun.

It's a strange and new experience to be among a group of individuals who are considered "distinct." I used to walk through a store without being noticed, but now it feels like I'm a celebrity. I can sense people looking at me and talking about me. It was quite unsettling the first time I went out in public after being in the hospital. Why were people suddenly paying attention to me? Why were they treating me differently? Is this how people react to those who are different? While I personally didn't feel it was because of my wheelchair, canes, limp, or oxygen use, I can empathize with those who may perceive it that way. I've witnessed people approaching my daughter, who has red hair, and asking if her hair color is real (one lady on a plane even requested to cut a piece off to show her hairdresser, which we declined!). I've seen people questioning my twin nephews, asking if they are twins, which one is which, and who's older. People's curiosity about differences can sometimes be off-putting, but in my case, I believe it stems from astonishment at the journey I've been through and survived. People also say that what I went through was a miracle, a gift from God, and seeing me affirms their faith and belief in prayers.

My family has shared with me that strangers now approach them and say, "You're Julie Brown's brother or sister, right?" That never used to happen to them. Many people followed our journey, saw pictures of our family, and now feel like they know us. It's a surreal experience for ordinary people like us. I recognize that without all those curious individuals, I wouldn't have had the army of prayer warriors supporting me during my recovery. I am grateful and humbled by everyone who inquired about me and prayed for me.

CHAPTER 16
MIRACLES DO EXIST

When people see me now, they often ask, "How are you? What's next?" The answer is simple - everything has changed, and it's all for the better!

I learned the power of hope from my friend, Melissa, during my time in the hospital. At first, I struggled to grasp the concept, but Melissa, who had faced her own health battles, guided me through it. Hope became my beacon in the darkness, showing me a path to a brighter future. It made my struggles more manageable and instilled in me the belief that better days were ahead. With hope as my driving force, I found the motivation to take each step forward. While I used to cringe at the idea that every challenge is an opportunity, I now see the truth in it. The aftermath of my battle with COVID presented me with numerous obstacles, but I chose to view them as chances for growth and pushed myself to overcome them.

My faith was put to the test during this journey. Believing in a higher power can be a challenging concept to fully embrace. Did I truly trust that God and his angels were looking out for me on this Earth? Weren't those who had passed on to heaven already enjoying eternal peace and rest after their time here? I can now confidently say that they are indeed watching over us from above! When I was in the hospital in the early days before being placed on a ventilator, I was overwhelmed with fear and seeking any guidance or support I could find. People advised me to surrender my worries to God and trust in His help.

Being quite literal, I struggled to understand how to do that. So, I turned to prayer, and as I continued to pray, I reached a point where I could no longer bear my burdens alone, and I surrendered my life to God. One night, lying in the hospital bed after trying every relaxation technique, I finally let go of all my concerns and said, "I'm done, I can't do this anymore." A sense of peace washed over me, and I heard a deep voice (though I can't recall the exact words) before drifting off to sleep. When I woke up the next morning, I felt a sense of relief. I have come to realize that we cannot control God's plan and that we do not have to face every challenge on our own. Life presents us with trials that can shake us to our core.

Maintaining faith helps to calm our anxieties and fears during tough times, teaching us to humbly accept support from others. While I was in the hospital, my sister Karen had a dream about our late Aunt Jane, who had passed away a few years earlier. In the dream, Aunt Jane was peacefully reading on a park bench when a man asked, "Who is responsible for watching over Julie tonight?" Aunt Jane closed her book and replied, "It's my turn," before coming down to sit by my hospital bed for the night. Whether this was a comforting dream for my sister or a message sent to her, we may never know. But the thought of loving departed family members returning to Earth to be with us in times of need is truly comforting.

Living in the moment was a valuable lesson I learned during this journey. The significance of each moment in life became apparent when faced with the possibility of not having any more. While confined to the hospital for days and weeks, I felt like I was missing out on precious moments with my kids, grandkids, family, and friends. It troubled me to see everyone else moving forward while I was stuck in a hospital bed. However, I realized the importance of creating my own moments. Every visit from someone, even if just for a couple of hours, became a cherished moment. Each card with words of encouragement was a special moment. Achieving milestones and setting new ones became moments to celebrate. The uncertainty of future moments made living in the present crucial. It was essential not to let life pass by but to actively create moments.

Surprisingly, some of the best moments of my life came from this challenging journey. I found gratitude in the experiences I wouldn't have had if I hadn't gotten so sick. The last conversation with Tom before being put on the ventilator, the one-on-one time with family and friends in the hospital, and the day I finally returned home were all moments I wouldn't trade for anything. It may seem strange, but I am somewhat grateful for the severity of my COVID illness. I have found a new sense of happiness and contentment in this transformed version of myself. I appreciate each day and what I accomplish, finding joy in life and all its offerings. Stress has dissipated, and I now spend more time outdoors, relishing in nature, fresh air, and the warmth of the sun on my face.

These simple pleasures were missed during my hospital stay, and I never thought I would experience them again. Before COVID, I don't think I was ever truly satisfied with my life. Now, I am eternally grateful and happy with the life I have. I begin and end each day with a moment of gratitude, which grounds me and sets a positive tone for the day.

When faced with a bleak future, it is crucial to practice patience. Upon receiving the doctors' recommendation for a lung transplant as my best option, I initially felt overwhelmed. However, I quickly embraced the decision and eagerly awaited the scheduling of the procedure to move forward. The days passed slowly as the medical team worked on the paperwork for Temple and navigated the steps required for acceptance into the transplant program. Tom advised me to take each day as it comes and not to focus too far ahead. His patience proved invaluable as we eventually discovered a less invasive healing path. This experience highlights the importance of patience in long-term recovery. Progress may seem slow, but rushing the process can lead to frustration. Developing patience is essential for enduring the challenges of a recovery journey.

My personal journey has instilled in me a deep sense of gratitude for life. It is all too easy to become consumed with the pursuit of personal improvement and overlook the blessings we already have. When life throws a curveball and forces us to pause, we are given the opportunity to reflect on our blessings and truly appreciate them. I am fortunate to have a supportive husband, loving children and in-laws, wonderful grandchildren, a close-knit family, lifelong friends, and a network of dedicated prayer warriors. I also have a fulfilling career, a comfortable home, an abundance of food, and a wardrobe filled with clothes.

In the past, I may have taken these blessings for granted and constantly sought more. However, I have come to realize the power of gratitude and its transformative effect on my outlook. Through this experience, I have learned to cherish the relationships with my family, friends, and community, and discovered the incredible support system that surrounds me. Gratitude has taught me that what I have is truly enough and that happiness stems from appreciating the present moment. Moreover, I have found joy in giving back to others, not just through material gifts, but by embodying positivity, resilience, and kindness.

Choosing to live with a positive mindset is a daily challenge, but the rewards are immeasurable. Positivity is contagious and has the power to uplift those around us. I have witnessed firsthand the impact of maintaining a positive outlook, as exemplified by my husband's unwavering commitment to focusing on the good even in challenging times. By embracing positivity and gratitude, we can cultivate a mindset that transcends obstacles and fosters a sense of abundance and fulfillment.

I experienced moments of anxiety and depression during my battle with COVID-19. There were times when I questioned why God allowed this to happen to me, moments when I feared being dependent on a ventilator in a nursing home for the rest of my life, and times when I felt guilty for surviving while others did not. I also struggled with the guilt of potentially passing the virus to my mother, who tragically succumbed to it. These negative thoughts weighed heavily on me and hindered my healing process. Thankfully, Tom was there to remind me to stay positive and take things one day at a time.

Over time, I came to realize that I couldn't blame God for my illness; it was a challenge I had to face. If others contracted the virus from me or did not survive, it was not my fault. I had to focus on overcoming my own struggles and embracing hope. I had a choice: I could dwell in self-pity or take action. I decided to take small steps towards recovery, celebrating each milestone and focusing on what I could do in the present moment.

While I may not return to my pre-illness self, I am committed to becoming the best version of myself moving forward. I have learned to appreciate each day and embrace my new "normal." It's about progress, not perfection. Today, I choose to celebrate the journey and cherish the present moment.

During our darkest moments, Tom and I felt the comforting presence of the Holy Spirit. In times of great distress, we found solace, warmth, and strength to keep moving forward. Though our challenges persisted, we felt a guiding presence accompanying us through each day, easing our fears and illuminating hope. We learned that we are never alone in our struggles. When fear grips you, seek strength from the Lord. The Holy Spirit may bestow its gift upon you or a loved one you pray for, bringing peace and solace. Trust in God and you may discover the peace you seek. Remember, angels are always ready to assist us; all we need to do is ask. In moments of need, humbly seek His guidance and support.

Before my experience with COVID, I rarely used the word "miracle" in my vocabulary. Many have described my survival as a miracle. But what exactly constitutes a miracle? If it signifies an intervention by God, then I do believe that my recovery from COVID was indeed a miracle. I am certain that divine assistance guided me through my darkest moments, indicating that it was not my time to depart from this world.

Can a miracle also serve as an inspiration to others? In that case, I have noticed that my journey has inspired many. It has reignited faith in those who were skeptical or had neglected their faith in their daily lives. It has prompted people to engage in daily prayer and has fostered a sense of compassion and empathy within our family. Individuals facing challenges now draw strength from my experience, much like how I and my family members drew inspiration from my father's battle with emphysema in his final years.

While I may not fully comprehend the nature of miracles or why one was bestowed upon me, I have come to realize that miracles are not meant to be understood but believed in. Trusting in the idea that God performs miracles strengthens our faith. I hope that all those in need of a miracle can find their path to a positive outcome, whatever form it may take.